The Twinflame Journey

The path to fulfillment within & understanding divine timing

D1518697

ALYSSA ASE

For more information, address:
breakingloveopen@gmail.com

First paperback edition June 2022

Book design by Alyssa Ase

ISBN (paperback) 979-8-83297-857-4
ISBN (ebook)

To my cat Keilla, my twinflame Jason,
and every single twinflame who shares this
age of Aquarius with me.

CONTENTS

INTRODUCTION

I usually hate introductions in books, so I will keep this short and sweet. I am a twinflame myself. I have always been driven by something in my heart and soul to find love within. I didn't know what that was for years. I knew I was guided away from what other people wanted for me. The more I shared with people, the more they argued with me about my actions or outlook on life. People made me believe something was wrong with me for a long time. Through spirituality, I have come to claim quite the opposite. I simply do not match up with the rest of society. Being a twinflame on top of being a spiritual outcast has given me the freedom to eventually accept myself for exactly who I am and reject what anyone else thinks entirely. Twinflames are not very common and hard to find, so I am so grateful for the community I have found on TikTok. There are many divine feminines there who spread positivity, hope and honesty about the journey. We poke a little at the divine masculines, but it is all good fun and, personally, I think keeps our spirits up. You aren't alone in this. It may feel like it at times, but you have a whole spirit team behind you and all the divine feminines spreading the message of love.

CHAPTER ONE

TWINFLAME FAQ's

she liked him. she did.
he had wild hair and an
old soul like hers and
somehow, she had fallen
tragically
in love
with his sad beautiful
eyes.

N.R. Hart
"sad.beautiful"

If reading that, you felt goosebumps or a sensation deep in your heart; you probably have a twinflame. It's hard to explain why you love this person. It's beyond you sometimes, and it's definitely beyond everyone you know. But you still can't let go of them. This person did something to your heart when you met them. It's like they stamped it with a code, and it will never disappear. The more you are away from this person, the more connected you feel to them. This has not been a normal relationship, and this person is not the average person you've been involved with either. You feel tied to them, and you can't move on no matter how hard you try.

You two have been in an on-again, off-again relationship; things have been rough and it's beat you both up pretty bad. And now, your counterpart has left you, ghosted you, or blocked you. You're sad and just want some answers why they would do this to you if they loved you. You cannot forget your twinflame, even if you try. You feel strongly for them, not like any other person you've been involved with. When you think deeply about them, even in separation, the feeling radiates through every cell in your body; you can feel them on your skin and in your bones.

This is like nothing else on earth. It's more potent than dopamine, the love drug that gets released into your body when you meet someone new. Dopamine eventually wears off when the honeymoon period ends, but the feeling of your twinflame never does. It just remains in your body permanently. There's no way to get rid of it, no matter how long you are separated from your counterpart. This is all because you are one soul. You are them; they are you. You cannot disconnect from it, and a cord-cutting will be useless in this situation.

This person was custom-created and designed to trigger you. This person is you, and they will reflect to you all your dark sides, trauma, wounding, and faults. It will be challenging to stay together and even more difficult to stay apart.

All of this matters because if you are at the point of reading this book, you are most likely in separation from your twin, and I will explain why you cannot contact them during a separation phase. After enough shit has gone down, possibly after many separations, one person will start running away from the relationship, and the other will begin to chase. In some scenarios, runners will later become chasers. They switch roles until one twin enters a spiritual awakening.

Everyone's tale looks different, and honestly,

when you hear about others, you may feel judgment come up. Another person's twinflame journey will never feel as special as yours, but I guarantee you, it is to them. This is an excellent opportunity to start looking at others without judgment and with total compassion. I find this easier to do within the twinflame community because we understand each other as no one else does.

The point of separation where your twin is running and won't talk to you—is the toughest point for most. If your twin is still at a point of trying to return to your life in the middle of a separation and they haven't healed or changed, then the universe feels you have more to heal and is smacking you with 2x4's. These are the lessons you must learn. It's not something to feel shame over; it is the universe's way of nudging you because you haven't been going in the direction it wants you to. If your counterpart isn't returning at this point – that is a good sign! Yes, that's what I said. It means #1; the universe feels you have done enough work that you don't need any more 2x4s to the head. This doesn't mean to stop working on yourself. Instead, it means you don't have to be dragged through the mud anymore. #2 It's a sign that the universe is now beginning to work on your counterpart. See chapter 3 for separation tips – these will help immensely. The more you do them, the more they benefit you.

The universe has a big project right now, in the age of Aquarius. There are 8 billion people on this planet now, and the awakening we will be experiencing for the next five years is the most relevant in history. It needs as many twins as possible to be in a whole, self-loving phase. Twins coming back into healed unions are a crucial way to show the collective how to heal. They will see our stories and the grief we went through and be encouraged to do healing work themselves, therefore not giving up on their partners so easily. This will bust the myth that people can't change and encourage people to do the work. If you have noticed in the collective right now, men have given up on women, women are pissed off at men, there are a ton of hurtful, traumatic actions going on in relationships, and we all know about the divorce rate. The words 'narcissist', 'drama', 'too emotional', and 'gaslit' cause even more hatred between the sexes and divide us further. All made up by society to keep us out of hearts and in our egos. As part of your spiritual ascension, you will eventually need to feel the importance of this mission in every cell of your body, just as you feel your twin. We are all one on this earth, and you have been brought to this specific human experience to teach others that.

All human experiences and twinflame journeys are very unique. That is why it is difficult to prove a person is your twinflame. If they are, buckle your seatbelt because this is not an easy journey, especially in the beginning. It will be the most fulfilling one if you pass all the tests the universe will give you. If you are on a twinflame journey where the contract says you will end in union, you are at the highest level of ascension and your last lifetime on earth. There is nothing more significant than love on this planet. It makes perfect sense that the most challenging journey would be equally as powerful.

The universe sets up situations so that everyone can learn how to love more profoundly and has no intention of making them feel bad about it. In other words, every situation is set up to learn how to overlook the 3D physical world.

How do you know if a person is your Twinflame, soulmate, or a karmic connection?

Usually, only time will reveal a twinflame

connection. The universe will show you if they are one. You may have already received confirmation. That could come in the form of messages from your spirit guides or a reading from a trusted intuitive or both. It's so intense to actually receive confirmation. The universe will continue to make this person a part of your life. You can try to deny it, avoid it, do cord-cutting ceremonies, hypnosis, therapy, or distractions. You can try to ask the universe to make this person leave your life, change your phone number, block them, or even move away. It won't matter. I tried most of these and my twinflame is still the biggest part of my life outside of my own pursuits.

A twinflame will be the catalyst and driver that sends you into a spiritual awakening. This will consume your life just like your counterpart does. Karmics can do this for some as well. A karmic is someone who can be mistaken for a twinflame but isn't one. If you dated a narcissist at some point, that would have been your karmic. Narcissists are here to wake a lot of us up. That's why so many women and men take their power back after dating one of these personalities. The major difference between a karmic and a twinflame is that you will stop loving a karmic. You might remember a few significant things about them, but everything else feels forgiven and forgotten.

The twinflame love goes so much deeper. It's almost like you are connected to every piece of them, including their inner child. You also can't see into a karmic's soul through their eyes, but a twinflame, you most definitely can. You can see all the pain they hold inside, and once that happens; you never forget it.

Because the twinflame journey is entirely spiritual, it will be based on the connection you have with your soul and your faith.

Soulmates are nowhere near twinflames. They typically don't experience separation. If they have a spiritual awakening, it won't be centered around the person they love. Soulmates are an easier connection. They just sort of click or match. And they are not for eternity. Because they are separate souls, at any time, they can split and move on from each other and mostly forget about each other. You can have many soulmates in life. They can come in the version of friends as well. But if you have a twinflame – there is only one.

Can you be happy in separation from your twin?

Before healing and ego death, this seems near impossible. Your programming and what you have been taught to believe keeps you in fear of the unknown. It keeps you loving a counterpart who couldn't show you love back. And guess what...that's not them; this isn't you. You didn't come here to suffer your entire life, nor did your counterpart. When will you take the leap of faith to jump to the other side? Ditch the fear. Be willing to let your counterpart go in the 3D so that you can feel your soul's love. You feel it with you first, and it feels incredible, then you remember you share your soul with counterpart and that real love was underneath all along. It can't be taken from you. The universe timed when you would see this message. It means you are ready.

Having a twinflame is not some cool romantic title you can use to follow a trend. Only your soul in contract with the universe decides if you are a twinflame. It's not something one personally selects just because they feel like it, and not everyone has a twinflame. Whether the two of you end up back in union is up to your soul contract.

Twinflame couples are like snowflakes; each one is incredibly different. Before you and your counterpart were born, your soul decided it would split into two human beings in this lifetime. In the soul contract, you picked your avatars, where you would live on the planet, where you two would meet. You also decided how this story would go between the two of you, what you will experience, the lessons you will learn, and the outcome. Once in separation, you will also start to see this is the sexiest person you have ever met. Sex with them was also the best you've ever had—all designed to keep you two tied to each other for life. There isn't much you can do to change this story, so this entire book is dedicated to getting you out of the stage of suffering and into a phase of happiness and fulfillment. Your soul and the universe would never pick something to hurt you. It is a temporary pain for the greater good of our collective here on planet earth.

What? I know, it sounds crazy. But crazy is a matrix-created word, and I will explain more about how you have been taught to abandon your soul and what you truly believe. That is the only thing that makes this journey hard beside the fact that you miss your counterpart. However, once you reset your neural pathways in your brain, missing them won't feel like the excruciating pain that it does now. It won't even feel like a dull ache. It will feel more like a knowing that mostly lives in your heart. I have been without my twin for almost three years. We've briefly connected two times. I know he will be back. Once you do the healing work and brain and ego work that I'm going to discuss in this book, you will understand that this isn't something that has been designed to punish you.

Can I leave the Twinflame Journey and be with a soulmate?

Yes, you have free will. When you are unclear about your purpose as a twinflame AND unclear about the purpose of separation from your twin, you will look for a way out, as well as, other options. It's natural because it's what you were taught to do. It's in your 3D operating system. Also, there are constant messages on social media showing people who found their person after having bad relationships or being treated poorly in the past. You will think you are one of those people. Not yet realizing you are a twinflame.

You may try to date. You may say you are going to give someone else a chance, but everyone will pale in comparison. Your friends who don't understand twinflames will tell you not to compare. They might insist you give someone else a chance. You don't yet comprehend that this person is a part of you. They live inside you, and you inside them. Dating will likely be unsuccessful. You'll have your standards high because you now know your worth, and yet no person will come along to meet them.

You will pretty much exhaust yourself with this until you give up. Eventually, you realize there is only one person you love and dating becomes this foreign thing you no longer understand.

One day, the universe will present you with someone who finally seems to meet your standards, just to see if you will go backwards. By that point, you will most likely understand more what your purpose is with the twinflame journey (see chapter 2), and you will find it impossible to be with a compatible soulmate.

If you are persistent in not surrendering to any of this, you'll never feel fulfilled. You'll never forget your twin. If you choose a partner, you'll eventually realize they'll never live up to your twin. They can't, they aren't your soul. They aren't the ones driving you to heal. They weren't written into your soul contract, primary storyline. They will eventually make you feel dead inside. This kind of feeling is another indicator that you are a twinflame and this is your person.

What is the runner thinking while they are running?

If you feel any kind of hurt or pain while reading this answer, it is indicative that you have a spot yet to heal. The answer is they aren't thinking about you very much. They are either focused on another person, work, or some other karmic lesson in progress. They are often numb to some kind of addiction. When running, your twin is asleep.

They haven't woken up to any of the deep knowing that you have. There is no spiritual awakening in sight yet. To them, the relationship just didn't work, and although they feel like they weren't 100% convinced they wanted to say goodbye to you, they also weren't willing to make an effort to stay. This is part of the process. You were also asleep at one point and didn't know anything about healing or spiritual awakenings. That is still where they are at. I speak from experience as I was once the runner. My twin and I were one of the rare twinflames where our trauma was so chaotic that we both experienced being the runner or chaser. We swapped roles later in our story. This happens so that you can see the hurt you have inflicted on your twin. If I ran from him first, he ran from me later. This is one way twinflames can mirror each other.

Runners aren't feeling and aren't thinking about the situation clearly. It will not become clear until the universe is ready to wake them up through karmic lessons. At some point, they will enter a spiritual awakening, and if you have surrendered to the journey as part of your soul contract, then they will realize there is something about you they have been denying. Basically, they fucked up. You cannot awaken them to this, and you can't make them see. It's just how it is.

You're Not a Twinflame; You Have Unhealed Attachment Issues
-OR-
You're not a Twinflame; You're Trauma Bonded
-OR-
This isn't a Twinflame Relationship; It Is Toxic

There is much controversy around twinflames, as people that don't understand the journey will say they are toxic couples who shouldn't be together. You may also hear they are abusive and making unsuspecting people stay in unsafe relationships. This is completely untrue.

If you haven't heard these statements yet, you most likely will at some point. They can be very confusing to most people. If twinflames didn't have trauma to heal, they would have been ready for a soulmate relationship. Soulmates may have work they do in their relationship, and they most likely still have inner growth work to do, but they aren't going to have the extreme triggering that twinflames have. Soulmates that don't have trauma to heal don't need separation because they communicate on the same level, without harm to one another.

When people say, 'You're not a Twinflame because your relationship had abusive circumstances. This person has no potential, ' they are unaware that abuse is caused by trauma. The Twinflame journey is about healing trauma on all levels. Spirit does not judge or discriminate...only humans do.

Twinflames are supposed to trigger each other. Those triggers identify which trauma needs to be healed. As I will mention more in Chapter 9, this is a journey you chose. You chose the type of trauma you would have and what you would have to do to overcome it. You chose the dynamic between you and your counterpart and exactly how that would play out.

The next question is, how do you know if this is a true twinflame or nothing but a toxic karmic relationship? In addition to spirit not letting you forget this person and your spiritual awakening being a non-stop consuming thing, there is one significant other difference. Your counterpart won't keep dragging you through toxicity. They will clarify that they don't like it even if they seem to be bonded to it. And they will eventually turn their backs on you. This is to protect you from it. This is to open up the avenue for you to work on yourself and examine every aspect of your life to remove any toxicity you have left. If you have addictions, gossip about other people, or are codependent, you open up too many possible pathways that allow toxicity into your life. It isn't just your twinflame that is toxic. You are mirrors, and you have both hurt each other. Whatever this trauma is, it's in you too. Many think they can throw their twin away, and the trauma will disappear as well. That's not true, and you will take your trauma with you wherever you go until it's dealt with. True twinflames will identify the toxicity within themselves and work on their own or with trauma professionals to release it from their lives. They won't do this in a relationship. They can't. Therefore, healing together is not part of the journey. Your twin isn't the only problem. You aren't innocent here. If they are considered to be toxic, you are too. If they are blaming you for things that aren't true, you are most likely also blaming them for things that aren't true.

It can be hard to see because the ego wants to blame. Ego doesn't want you to look within. Ego doesn't want you to change. And society, in general supports blaming another person rather than looking within. You can see this through the huge narcissist movement. When women started identifying their exes as narcissists without even having any expertise in diagnosing such a thing, it opened up an opportunity for them to stay in the victim stage. Is it healthy to be a victim for a short period of time in order to help you identify why a certain situation or relationship wasn't good for you? Yes. Is it good to stay there? No. Remaining a victim prevents going within to see how that partner was attracted to begin with. Narcissists usually attract empaths. Empaths want to heal others and through the empath's eyes, narcissists are the perfect people for this because they have so many issues that haven't been worked on. It creates this strong attraction because there is so much to fix. The immature empath will keep getting involved with this type of person over and over again because they haven't worked on their codependency issues or put boundaries in place. Heal these and the attraction to the narcissist will fade. It's really that simple.

A very important thing to know regarding twinflames is that there are often two categories of them. One set of twinflames did not abuse each other, they weren't mean to each other but still go into separation. The second set of twinflames were mean to one another and experienced an intense relationship that borderlines abuse in some way. Because there are two sets, you will find some twinflame coaches who insist twinflames are never abusive to each other. When you are in the second category, you can find yourself wondering once again, if this is your twinflame. This is why I have decided to specialize in coaching and providing information to twinflames who experienced borderline abuse with their counterparts.

I want to make it clear that I don't condone staying in a toxic relationship. There are some who choose to use the twinflame title as an excuse to stay with an abusive partner. This is not what the twinflame journey is about and those are not actual twinflames. A twinflame leaves their unhealed counterpart alone once they have a clear understanding that they need to heal. Before then, they may not be fully awake and may still be trying to make a relationship work. There's not much that can be done about this. You can't force anyone to see or heal before they are ready. But you must realize the twinflame journey is a spiritual one. If people in the matrix are trying to spiritually bypass by using this title when they shouldn't, you can let that stop you from proceeding with your mission.

In a nutshell, it doesn't really matter how bad the relationship with your twin was. Put that in the past where it belongs, forgive and move forward with the person you are meant to become.

Do all Twinflames come into Union?

This isn't a yes or no answer and no one on earth can provide you with this answer. Either the universe or one of your spirit team members will give you answers. There is a reason this isn't clear as day for anyone. Everyone is on a different journey, so there may be souls reincarnated as twinflames who are supposed to learn a lesson from their twin, heal and move on to a soulmate. My belief is that these souls wanted part of the experience, but weren't an old enough soul that was ready to go to the final challenge of attaining union.

If you purchased this book, I would tell you that you most likely fall into the second category—the twinflames who are ready for the entire mission. That entails meeting your twin, then separating from this person you love more than anyone else. You find you cannot stop loving them, which then takes you on the journey to inner work, healing, and unconditional love. This faith-based mission is where there is no choice but to strip away all of your ego. To form a relationship with uncertainty. To BELIEVE.

There are more obstacles to overcome on this journey. There are intelligent machines and non-player characters (NPCs) trying to get in your way of union to see how firm you are in your belief of it. Watch Matrix Resurrections, the movie, because they will show you exactly what I am talking about. Trinity, is the twinflame of Neo. She doesn't contact him in the 3D, and she acts like she barely knows him when he tries to speak with her. But beneath the surface, she knows who he is. She's waiting for him to awaken before she will acknowledge him and the connection. If you are in separation, THIS is where you are at. Your divine masculine is Neo and the universe is putting them through various exercises before they get woken up entirely to the matrix, to their spiritual awakening, and to the twinflame journey, and you. You are to remain undercover like Trinity until your divine masculine wakes up.

Whether you are supposed to come into union with your twin can only be answered by you. Sit quietly and ask yourself the following questions:

- Are my twin and I meant to be together?
- Am I the only real person for my twin?
- Are they the only real person for me?
- Does this person make me want to make myself and the world better?
- Do I believe nothing can keep us apart forever, that this is only temporary?

Feel into your heart on these. When reading these questions, do you feel yourself saying 'Fuck YES' to each and every one of them? Then welcome to set of twinflames that are meant to come into union in this lifetime.

How do I let go of my Twinflame

without giving up?

You can't give up on your twinflame. Letting go without giving up is the exact definition of surrendering. When you surrender to the twinflame journey, you say to the universe:

- I believe in this, I believe in me, I believe in my twin
- I will go with the flow of the universe. Wherever I feel I am being pulled, I will go; I will not resist
- I will stop listening to unsolicited advice from others. I understand that they will never know me, my life, or my mission as I do
- I will commit to those things that will allow me to heal, awaken and ascend
- When the universe makes my purpose clear, I will make that my life
- I will forgive my twin and understand that they are asleep, and this is part of the journey
- I will set boundaries with everyone where necessary, even with my twinflame.
- I will stop looking for proof of my connection with my twinflame
- I will accept that I need to go through multiple

dark nights of the soul to strip away my ego and change my life

What is detaching, how do I do this?

I will discuss detaching without actually using the word itself throughout this book. Detaching never means you stop loving your twinflame. It never means you give up hope of union or believing whatever you want to believe about the two of you. It does mean to stop wanting the 3D relationship as badly as you have. Especially the one that got you to the point of separation. Let that go. Let your twin, as they are right now, go. Focus on everything that pertains to you. Make yourself the love of your life. This sounds foreign right now, but you will fall in love with yourself and the life you create. You know all those things in life you put off because your twin didn't want to do them or you weren't ready? DO THEM!!! Nothing is stopping you, but you.

How do you detach? You stop waiting on your twin. You let go of all that codependency that is holding you back in stupid ways. You stop focusing on #couplegoals. That is usually codependency, where one person is unhappy in that dynamic. This is precisely what twinflames are here to educate the world on. You see how we were born alone; we die alone and despite what you have been taught, we spend a ton of time alone in life. You create a whole relationship with yourself. If you rarely talk to other people, all the better. I understand we are tribal, and human connection is part of our existence. You don't have to let that die completely, but other people should not be taking up the majority of your time. When they do, you only exist as their idea of you, and you never find out who YOU really are.

Does Everyone Have a Twinflame?

Most people will answer this as yes. My answer is no. The common answer is – *Yes, though you might not meet them in this lifetime. Contrary to popular belief, you will not necessarily end up in a relationship with them in every incarnation because it is not always necessary.*

The reason I say no is because my particular definition of a twinflames is one soul split into two and reincarnated in the same lifetime. They will meet, they will separate, and they will heal. And some will reunite. They will cause each other to go through a spiritual awakening. If it's open it up to the other answer above, then people who aren't twinflames may spend their life LOOKING for their twinflame. The universe will make it known if you have a twinflame and need to be on a twinflame journey. All other information is going down an unnecessary rabbit hole.

Why can't I heal alongside my twin?

The Twinflame Journey is designed to create union within first. This is the highest-level ascension soul contract there is. It's challenging and it's supposed to be that way. The rewards are like nothing a soulmate couple will ever see. Why? Because you did it yourself. You steer clear of codependency on all levels. You want your twin to heal. It will drive you nuts that you can't see what's going on with them, but it has to be this way so you can focus on yourself. We can't wait for them to step into their full spiritual roles and to work with the universe in the ways we are. But their timeline isn't going to match yours. My twin in particular does everything I do 5-7 years behind me. I believe there was a purpose in our soul contract being that way. So, I could write this book, coach Twinflames, and be a content creator spreading love to anyone who will watch. Your soul contract has something incredible written it in as well. If you were distracted by your twin, you'd likely miss it. Do you want average or incredible? Separation is to benefit you, then benefit both of you in the future. Your relationship with the universe always comes before your twin and there will be times you will have to set boundaries with them for your higher good.

The problem with trying to wake up your counterpart before they are ready is that spirituality on this level seems to be Greek to them. They may listen to you, but won't hear you. Divine feminines go first in healing. Everything about divine feminines is designed to make us the leaders of stepping into the heart. Anytime a divine feminine tries to contact a divine masculine while they are running, they will most likely get pushed away again. This is a good opportunity to sit with that pain. This is where your faith needs to kick in. So, they can look you dead in the eyes and say they feel nothing; then you should be able to look past that and say, 'I know this is an illusion.' The universe is testing you. Will you believe even when your twin won't validate your feelings? You must pass. This journey is backward from everything you were taught before. You don't need anyone else to feel love. Love lives inside you, but the matrix has taught you to seek love externally. You are taught to please others, thinking you will gain love from them. They make you forget you already had it. It leaves you feeling drained and rids you of your happiness. Any person that tries to provide you with love you can't find on your own will also become drained. They, too are human, with their own issues in life, and cannot forever provide for another person in that manner. You need to be able to say to yourself repeatedly 'I have all I need inside; this is the only love I can forever depend upon; no one else needs to provide that to me.' Then your partner can feel free, and you can feel free as well. You get to have love and enjoy your life to the fullest.

What are divine vs. wounded masculine and divine vs. wounded feminine? How do these energies affect Twinflames?

The divine is the healed conscious masculine or feminine. The wounded is the programmed, traumatized, reactive, and toxic masculine or feminine. To get a better idea, here are some traits of each:

Wounded Masculine
Abusive   Controlling
Jealous.   Possessive
Avoidant   'Nice Guy'
Intimidating   Unstable
Aggressive   Lies.   Defensive
Competitive to the extreme

Wounded Feminine
Insecure   Codependent
Manipulative   Needy
Victim. Mindset
Inauthentic
Overly Emotional

Divine Masculine
Supportive   Vulnerable   Logical
Humble   Deeply Present   Centered
Assertive   Focused   Protective
Can hold space for others
Doesn't judge   Resilient
Protects their boundaries
Supportive   Confident   Honest

Divine Feminine

Vulnerable   *Open*   *Trusting*
Creative   *Empathetic*   *Authentic*
Receptive   *Flows through life*
Magnetic   *Intuitive*
Compassionate
Supportive   *Surrendered*

These lists are the best reference tool to show what we are to leave behind as we heal and what we want to step into as we ascend. When we become aware of our unhealthy patterns, and of our wounded self, we can stop recreating the same patterns, stop projecting them onto others, and heal our relationships. The twinflame relationship at the beginning has a lot of these wounded aspects. Codependency and attachment issues are the biggest ones that cause concerns.

Masculine and feminine are not gender-specific. You have both feminine and masculine in you, and so does your twin. What is truly fascinating about twinflames is the timing around how each one awakens in relation to one another. The stories will vary a little, but here, in a nutshell, is what happens:

The masculine counterpart will start to

avoid/ghost/block/run. The feminine counterpart chases until they can't anymore. They begin to realize that the masculine counterpart is set and determined to separate themselves from the feminine. At that point, the feminine stops and walks away, realizing on a conscious level that they are abandoning themselves by continuing to chase the masculine. This is your inner divine masculine waking up. The default nature of the divine feminine is to nurture, love, and be all-encompassing. The feminine seeks union. If only your inner divine masculine is awake, you will likely run; if your inner divine feminine is awake at the same time, you will begin to feel balanced. You stop chasing and become fully aware of both sides of the situation. You fully surrender to the Twinflame Journey.

Surrender means simply turning away and leaving the Universe to walk with your twin. You know better than to chase at this point. You recognize it is counterproductive. In many cases, the runner or divine masculine counterpart is only running from the chaser. Once the chasing has stopped, the runner has an opportunity to stop, take stock and reconsider. It can take a long time for the runner to realize that the chaser has stopped and when they do, they may feel lost and alone and perhaps wonder why. Eventually, they may seek their twinflame again, but only with divine timing. Only when it is meant to happen as monitored by the universe.

If both parties have not woken or healed enough, a false union will occur and then go back into separation again. My past unions failed because I thought I could carry all the weight for my twin and me. If I could just remain calm and relaxed, he can't affect me, and things will be fine. But the universe will see right through this. Only a true harmonious union will occur when the universe can see that both parties are on a playing field where they will respect one another.

How long will separation be for?

There's no timeline on this. Separation is based on the following:

#1 What you and your twin, as one soul chose would be the timeline, at the contract signing before reincarnation. You wanted to experience certain things in this lifetime in order to ascend. Those things all have to be checked off the list in the form of lessons. Don't kill yourself trying to heal, thinking it will speed up your counterpart's healing and therefore union. It won't. Part of your healing process is allowing yourself the grace and time to evolve without pressuring yourself along the way. This is where you need to learn to put yourself above union.

#2 You have free will, which means you and your twin may cause delays in getting to union. This can show up in the following ways:

- You or your twin is stubborn about healing when spirit urges you to
- You try to push the other person to heal or try to reveal things to your twin out of desperation for love
- There is resistance surrendering to the journey and the lessons that come with it

I feel confused. Why is everyone's version of the Twinflame journey

something different?

If you are searching the internet, you are probably confused about multiple things regarding twin flames, and what you are supposed to do next. Let me shed some light on these things so you can relax more on this journey.

EVERYONE'S OPINION WILL DIFFER!

Twin flame coaches exist to help us on this journey and it would be hard to find your way without the maps they provide. Do soak up as much information as you can from them, but do not take everything they say as your absolute truth. If they have made a statement that immediately doesn't feel right inside you, then make your own decision around what does feel right for you. Your inner voice should always override any guru.

If you watch enough twin flame coaches or intuitives, you will start to see that they all differ in the signs they have as to whether this is your twin flame:

*Twin flames always end in union

*Twin flames rarely end in union

*You aren't a twin flame if you don't end in a mission together

*You must feel an instant connection with them the minute you meet them

*You can channel their feelings

*You will have a Kundalini Awakening

I could probably list 20 or so more of these variances. It's overwhelming. To make it worse, the videos with the clickbait 'Signs this is your twin flame' titles can keep you on YouTube all day, hell, all week long, but they will also confuse you and send you right back to square one in your questioning. This is what I call the twinflame rabbit hole.

This is extremely important because if you get too wrapped up in the specifics, you will end up denying your twin flame journey and delay your spiritual ascension out of pure frustration.

Here is the thing you need to understand. The gurus and social media here on Earth will give you the perspective of what one person has experienced on their specific journey. They have not gone out to interview 10,000 twin flames to see the accuracy of what they are talking about. And that would be impossible because there are many people who think they have a twinflame and they don't, so how would you know whom to interview anyway? Exactly. So, the people online speaking about twin flames are doing their best based on the information they have to go on but should provide a disclaimer that it is from their experience and perspective. I was determined to deny my twin flame, and the universe directed me right back to where I had been months before with additional confirmation. All this is unfolding just as it should. Don't be upset at yourself for getting off track, and in fact, I invite you to deny this person is your twin and see what the universe does. That is how you get confirmation.

Confirmation can come in different ways. Your spirit guides/source may tell you why this is happening. When you think about your twin and explicitly try to let go of them, there may be a feeling running through your body that confirms the connection. You don't experience this with anyone else, just your twin. You will be led down different paths that you wouldn't normally go on your own. These things may have interested you before, but now there is a flashing neon sign telling you to go towards them. And, of course, certain things that other twin flames or twin flames coaches say will ring true. Just don't focus on the parts that don't.

In regards to the bullet points above, for my twin flame journey:

- I firmly believe we will end in union
- I had to do healing work before I could proceed to learn non-duality, 5th dimension & ego/mind control
- We may not be in mission together, most

likely individual missions helping the collective

- I did not feel an instant connection with him as I do now
- I can channel his feelings and purpose but have not yet experienced telepathy two ways

Your twin flame journey is unique and will differ from mine in some ways. Go to YouTube or google and search for twin flames and see what pops up for you. The universe has control over what you see and when you see it. 'When the student is ready, the teacher appears.' Get intimate with that saying because it is so true.

If you want to be with your twin flame, stop looking at what is tangible or third dimension (my twin flame and I are in or out of union, we are talking or are not talking, labels, etc.) and start looking beyond. Twin flames are all about the soul. You can't see it. It is a knowing. It is faith. Stop beating yourself up about wanting to be with them or thinking of them, and don't let others tell you how to feel about this person. You have to go within. What interests do you have around growth? Whatever comes up, go there. Boundaries, plant medicine, awakening retreats, letting go of co-dependency, breakup courses, childhood trauma work, shadow work, and inner child work all kept calling me. It might be different for you, but explore what you feel a pull to. Don't shut that intuition down. There are twin flame coaches who clearly state we don't need to heal and we should just go directly to learning non-duality. Disclaimer: If the universe has designated that you need to heal first, you need to heal first. Going straight to non-duality may have worked for one coach, but for others, that could be considered spiritual bypassing and can massively harm the psyche, and some of these cases have ended in suicide. I just can't stress enough to listen to your intuition. It took me three years to heal, and I would not have skipped a second of that just to get my twin back faster. The only thing that can make this train go faster is to stop resisting.

Another thing that will help you is defining for the universe how you want to be in a relationship with your twin. For example, you don't want them to be able to push your buttons, you want to have them in your life without getting lost in the relationship, and you want to be able to love fully, without attachment. Once you clearly state your intentions to the universe, it will devise a plan to deliver those things to you. You will have to experience the dark before you get to the light. The further you ascend, the more dark nights of the soul you will encounter. The universe knows what you truly want underneath it all. It can feel those wants and intentions.

One last note - many people, state that union is not the purpose of this mission. Indeed, the outcome of being with your twin is not the mission. If it were, the whole thing would be more straightforward, like it is for soulmates. The mission is your growth or spiritual ascension. However, we are humans who only do things we are driven to do. Are you going to go to work if they don't pay you? Are you going to shovel snow or mow lawns for your entire neighborhood just because? Absolutely not. Union is your motivation. Once you stop resisting that, everything begins to flow. Happiness, security, positivity, and a knowing of how to be in a relationship with your twin. What you resist will persist. Why not just sign on and see the magic happen?

CHAPTER TWO

WHAT IS THE PURPOSE OF TWINFLAMES?

If they build a wall…I will climb over it…

If they run… I will chase them down…

This is now or never for me….

I will spend every living day…on reaching my purpose, my goal….

And I will not let anything take away what is destined for me….

I am taking control of my life, and I am taking responsibility for my destiny…

I have traveled thousands of miles through hell…

And now I stand at the end of all and say if I die for this…. Then so be it

But I will not betray my heart anymore…

I will not let what the darkness has stolen escape my grasp….

I will not surrender, I will not retreat, this is my calling….

The burning pain inside me that wakes me up at night…. That is my guide…

It says to me… Every moment I don't spend pursuing my goal… I am wasting my breath…

Years I have trained myself for this final battle….

Years I have spent readying myself to walk through the fire…

Years I have spent to build a warrior out of myself…

And now…. It is time…

To do what is necessary…. To do what needs to be done…

And so if you feel this burning flame inside you….know that is your soul telling you to move towards your dream, your vision and to honor your heart….

No more waiting…. No more silence…

It is ours now to take….

For those of you who feel the same as I….let's start taking action and do not retreat…

Fuck the feelings and the fear…you find a way around the obstacles they have placed down…. And you go fight for them…. Fight until you have won….

No more hiding in the shadows….

I was born for this battle… And win the victory that was promised

~ Spiritual Ascension,
Posted by Brendan on Quora

I saw a TikTok of a young girl showing an old video of her boyfriend that had passed away. It was the two of them dancing in her bathroom. She had a ghosting effect layer to indicate this was a memory. She was clearly showing her viewers how happy they had been when they were together. In the background is another video layered behind the first one. Standing in the same room, is her, in present-day, in a nightgown, looking sad. The sound she chose for the video made me instantly feel her grief.

It reminded me of how I feel I've lost someone important to me I got curious and viewed more of her videos. What I found out was that he had been gone about six months. She had other videos about his passing away and still had many TikTok's posted from when he was alive. In one of the latter videos, she showed a scenario of how miserable she felt alone and how she only felt happy when he was there with her.

She reminded me why Twinflames are here. We lose our counterparts to learn not to be codependent on someone else for our happiness. We learn how to detach and how to set boundaries. This girl was with her boyfriend for eight months, a typical honeymoon phase for a relationship, and she was only 17. Six months later, she is still destroyed because she has never learned the things Twinflames learn in separation. She never learned to be happy by herself. And now she is living in pain because she believes the dopamine she felt when she was with him is the only way to feel fulfilled and happy. But it would never have been sustainable for him to make her happy forever. She exists in the 3D illusion of love.

Most people don't want to look at these facts; they just want to keep believing in the fairytale. Her video went viral—over one million likes. Society is in love with codependent love. Start watching social media closer. You will see videos, quotes and memes where one person is providing love for someone who can't seem to provide it for themselves. And that media will get more views and more likes than a person who has posted about finding love within. There's not even a space in our culture for ceremonies of the day one finally wakes up and declares self-love. But if a man has professed his love instead, we have weddings with multiple parties even if 50% of marriages end in divorce. Self-love lasts forever, but it doesn't get validated or acknowledged by our society.

You may think having a twin flame is just about

you and your counterpart and the union you desire between you, but it is more than that. We are here to show the entire collective how they have been misled. Either through Disney or through parents who only approve of a child who gets married. These messages are constantly passed to us. They are disguised as romance and security. But when you translate them, they say, 'You are worthless if someone else doesn't declare their love for you,' 'You are worthless if you don't get married,' and 'If you remain single, there is something wrong with you.' Love becomes an achievement rather than an expression of our hearts. Even couples in successful relationships are constantly badgered about when they will get married. And if the man takes longer to propose because he needs to prove to himself that he can provide for her, <u>she</u> is shamed by society. People will tell her to realize that he doesn't love her without knowing any other details.

Everything is pressure and on a timeline. Then people focus more on their wedding day than if the marriage will even work. They get wrapped up in parties and gifts and how big the diamond ring is on their finger. And if that marriage ends, they immediately try to look for all those same external things with someone else. Watch Jennifer Lopez. She is a prime example. She is currently on her sixth engagement and soon to be fourth marriage at the time of the publishing of this book. The rings are all amazing. She's the best looking 52-year-old we've ever seen. People are envious of her, watching her like crazy in the tabloids. So, if everything in her life is so perfect, why can't she keep a relationship? Because she doesn't love herself and doesn't know how to be happy on her own. As one breakup happens, she is on to the next within a month or so. She doesn't date slowly; she gets engaged quickly. She loves the high of how that person makes her feel because she can't recreate that feeling in herself.

So, what has this got to do with Twinflames, your separation, and having no idea when union will happen? I'll answer that in more detail, but first, let's look at what happens to twinflames and their stages. All journeys are different, so I will keep this to the part the divine feminines go through.

#1 Honeymoon stage with your counterpart, just like normal relationships

#2 Relationship struggles, which may include many on-again, off-again periods

#3 Finding out this is your twinflame probably around the same time as one of the more severe separations

#4 A feeling of needing to heal yourself or work

on yourself along with an unexpected spiritual awakening. (This may be interchanged with step 3 for some divine feminines).

#5 Finding out you can't make it past the first date with anyone else. If you haven't made it to this stage yet, or are still trying to date, you'll find out that eventually, these attempts are futile and ineffective. It's not that you are comparing them to your twin. Your twin holds a gigantic space in your heart even when they haven't been the best partner or even a remotely good one. This is your first glimpse of unconditional love.

Steps 3 (separation) and Step 5 (not being able to move on) prevent you from doing what Jennifer Lopez does. Even if Ben Affleck himself or any celebrity you find attractive walked into your life, you would still not be able to let them in. So, now you are alone. The spiritual awakening has probably caused you to lose many of your friends, causing you to spend even more time alone. You spend more time doing healing work than anyone you know. You read books like this trying to understand what the fuck this journey is about. The people talking about how you picked someone emotionally unavailable and therefore do not love yourself taunt you more than ever. At first, reading about twinflames seems fascinating, but that gets old, and then you want real answers on how to fix this and get back into union. You can't just talk to your counterpart, though, because they are likely not to respond, or speak with you briefly, then run or outright block you. Jesus, you are stuck! You have no choice whatsoever other than to look at yourself. Your twin seems to have shown you all the things inside of you that sabotage your life. You want to return to blaming them; it's so much easier. You successfully stay angry for longer than you ever could have imagined. So mad that you want to tell them to stay out of your life forever. But even if you tell them, do they listen? Nope, they return right when you set boundaries with yourself. You can't say no to this person. Why not, are you crazy? You turn to healing work to deal with your attachment issues and practice affirmations. You sign up for therapy and every online class you can get your hands on. You are determined to get over this person. Maybe the next course and a few weeks will be all that is needed. You will surely forget your twin this time. But it never happens, no matter how much money you spend on this stuff. Your counterpart consumes your thoughts every morning, day, and night. You wish to find a new partner, but your twin is living rent-free inside your heart.

Welcome to being a twinflame. This whole experience, including the time alone, the healing work, and the self-reflection, gives you no choice but to change. Your ego will fight it every single step of the way, making it take longer, but there isn't another way. It's one path, and the more you resist it, the fiercer the universe gets with you. You will become a whole new person from this experience. Your addictions will slowly be removed from your life. You will start pursuing things you always wanted to but never could, possibly out of fear. You will slip backward a few times, but eventually, when you do enough things for yourself, things that make you feel good or passionate about your life, you begin to feel a light inside. What is that? You only ever felt that when another person made you feel it. Wait, what? But there is no one else around. You've been doing everything by yourself. Is this…it can't be…is this your own light? Is this self-love? Has that been in there all along? Seriously?

Yes, my loves. That was what was hidden from you when people taught you that only a partner could make you happy in life. The twinflame journey and your counterpart's actions provide you with the freedom that every person on this planet should have. No codependency, no attachments, fewer disappointments, and less suffering in life. Why? Because you don't have to ask or wait for another person to provide these for you. When frankly, most of the time, they can't anyway.

Your past pattern has been to focus on your partner; therefore, you'd rather have your counterpart back and forget all these things that will lead to independent happiness. Letting go of that and slowly graduating to something you enjoy will eventually get you to the place of inner light. It's not rocket science, and you don't have to be one of the special ones. This is human nature, plain and simple, inside all of us.

So back to the twinflame purpose and the collective. You are or will be an example. The universe pushed you to experience all of this on your mission so that you would teach others. You can be the new model that shows how someone can be happy on their own. When you come back into union, the collective will listen to you even more because they will be fascinated by your story. Don't forget; they are captivated by romance and a tale of how two people broke apart and then came back together. For God's sake, every rom-com movie is that same story. You will have their ears and a chance to say; that you came back together only because you found your inner love. You will be one of those people that preach how you cannot love someone else until you fully love yourself. Or you can make this your life purpose. Educate other twinflames about coming back into union or teach the whole damn collective. You don't have to wait for union for that either. In my opinion, divine feminines are learning more from other divine feminines still in separation than those in union.

DUALITY

This planet with the human species was created to experience duality and it only exists in your lifetimes on this planet. Non-duality just is, like love is just singular; there is no opposite. With duality, everything has an opposite, love vs. fear, good vs. bad, the dark vs. the light, etc. You came here just to experience this. In other words, how would you know what love really is if you couldn't experience its opposite?

We know twinflames came here for a challenge. The whole entire story is part of the challenge. The bad times we experience when we were little, being heartbroken by relationships and losing our twin. It's all part of love being taken from us, so we could appreciate it. You didn't choose to suffer; you chose to experience. There is a massive difference.

Twinflame ascension is a spiritual awakening on steroids. It's a fast track to awakening to your soul's truth. When you meet your twin, or sometime after that, possibly in separation, you'll be thrown into it whether you want it or not. What can take years and years to work through in a normal, gentle awakening can be done in just a few months, precisely because it is a twinflame spiritual awakening. All of your past trauma, your shadows, and lessons will come up for you to review in a somewhat forced way.

The twinflame connection is not for the faint of heart. The energy between the two of you is intense, and by just being in their presence, you'll become aware of parts of yourself you didn't know were there, nor do you want to look at. It's about so much more than romance. The twinflame journey targets raising the human collective's vibration, which you and your counterpart do, separately healing your wounds, working through karma, and learning life lessons.

Meeting your counterpart pushes you and gives you the motivation to do this work. It is absolutely brutal facing these shadow parts of yourself and admitting you need to change, and this is why many say they want off the twinflame ride. By doing this work separately and alone, you raise the collective's vibration while also aligning with your twin. Once aligned, your energy will be more balanced when you're together. No matter how hard it gets, you're always connected to them energetically, and what your soul planned before reincarnation will come to fruition.

Your twin doing what they are doing is the universe checkmating you. You see, you have avoided your healing and your true purpose for so long...the universe said buzz...times up. Guess what...you aren't here to be part of the matrix in the way others are. People who are asleep are slaves to the matrix...they get torn apart by it when everything doesn't go perfect. This is what society has done to us. You must be a size 2. You must always look young. You must be Instagram-worthy. You must have a 2 to 10-carat diamond on your ring finger, and most importantly, a man. You must be a slave to the competitiveness of #couplegoals, Valentine's Day, or 'Happy wife, happy life'. The matrix has taught you that you should be married, with a successful 9-5 job and two kids by age 30, or something is wrong with you. You must have a lavish wedding and a partner with no boundaries, willing to do just about anything for you. It's a never-ending cycle leaving everyone feeling worthless. To have a partner for show or to feel better about ourselves is not love. That's programming. Only about 10% or less of couples are actually happy. Why? Because they were taught that it is the other person's responsibility to make them happy. They never learned how to find it within themselves first. They make the other person in the relationship miserable because that person can NEVER provide love for someone who doesn't know how to love themselves.

Your soul has spared you from those ridiculous, basic lessons, and you get to go within and connect with who you really are. Your twin is running from you because you are not being the real you. The one that exists at the soul level. You are your programming, and you were trying to get them to be part of your subconscious programming. This shows up through expectations, demands, codependency, lack of boundaries and insecurities. People still get into relationships like this and then divorce later or live in an unhappy marriage for eternity.

Your twin runs from you because they don't want that. They don't want five years with you and a messy divorce. That's entanglement and bondage. Twinflames at the soul level are free all the time. They are at peace all the time. Your twin left you so that you could find that. It's not that they want to love anyone else, but they want to experience you while you are both as close to a soul level as possible. When you try to control anything, you are not your soul, you are not peace, and you are not freedom. You don't work on these things. You become them.

The Twinflame journey is misunderstood. We aren't here to care about chasing someone at all. Mature divine feminines understand that separation forces us to heal, find empowerment & self-love within ourselves. Once we get to a point where we no longer obsess over the masculine or union, we do help others. We introduce to the entire collective that love is not what the matrix taught them. That is all fake love and has been proven unachievable, as shown by the divorce rate and the statistics around the couples who stay together but aren't even happy together.

Have you ever stopped to examine if your desires in life are really <u>your</u> wants or if they were programmed into your subconscious? In working past subconscious programming, you work past your issues with love, and find yourself so that you can bring this message to all. Be free of the system.

Divine feminines are sent into separation and continue to love their counterparts without social constructs. That should feel good, not sad…that's REAL LOVE. You aren't controlling your divine counterpart; you don't need something from them. You simply just love…pure unconditional love. For every one of you who turns your back on society…you are making a difference. You are changing the world.

There's a secret to the Twinflame journey. You have to form a relationship with uncertainty. You must do what it takes and trust that the universe will bring you your twin. Every single part of the matrix is telling you this won't happen. It wants to win; it wants you to choose the easy way. Pick another karmic, pick a soulmate; is that what you want?

When your twin consumes your love and your heart? When you feel them every morning when you wake up and every night when you go to bed?

Ever heard the Brene Brown quote that says, 'If you're not in the arena also getting your ass kicked, I'm not interested in your feedback?' It's you in the arena getting your ass kicked for love. No one else needs to understand that. You become a person who has fully healed their trauma and learned self-love the way the universe pushes you to. You will KNOW EXACTLY what unconditional love means. It will flow through you. Twinflames are the example to the rest of the world, and that should never be taken lightly or judged by someone who has never felt what we feel.

I'm going to tell you one very personal thing about my Twinflame journey. Six years ago, my twin stood in my living room in tears as I pushed him away; he asked me why I couldn't see he was hurting. Now he acts like that never happened. He completely buried that pain. It haunts me. It haunts me to a point where I feel I need to succeed…at love, at my dreams, in my purpose. He is there in every part of me, driving me forward.

The universe is asking you to look within, to do the work. If the universe selected you as a divine feminine Twinflame, you have a vital role in showing this world currently full of war and pandemics that love overrides everything...even your own uncertainty. What will you choose?

The final reason you are on this journey is to fast-track healing generational trauma. Through your healing work, you not only heal it for past lines of your ancestors but also stop the train and not pass onto any children you may have. There are other starseeds in the collective that have signed up for this, but twinflames are more drawn to do this than anyone else through the absolute magnetic love and pain they feel about their twin. Those who are here to break generational trauma and ties will feel a heavy, heavy weight. It's not meant to be easy, and this job is your chosen job. Your ancestors before couldn't do it. Their souls weren't ready to ascend, but yours is.

CHAPTER THREE

WHY SEPARATION IS A BLESSING, NOT A PUNISHMENT

Right off the bat, nothing seems good about separation from your twinflame. Not being able to speak with and see the person you love most in the world? Especially if you are new to separation, you will think this is the worst idea. It's hard and sad, and you don't want to get out of bed before noon if you don't have to. When you haven't done much healing work, haven't gone through all the change needed in your life yet, you feel dead inside without your twin; the longing is so great, it seems unbearable. Yes, separating from your twin can be devastating and painful — but it probably needed to happen.

If you are in the first few weeks of separation, you probably think your divine masculine will reach out to you next week. Or maybe it's just like the no-contact websites talk about? 30 days, you'll just give it 30 days and they will be back. That's not actually how this goes. Some separations will be 8-9 months and some will be 8-9 years. It's quite common to hear of these timeframes and want to take this book and throw it at the wall. That's normal. If you have not yet seen the advantages of separation, you will tend to feel hopeless and start to wish you never met this person. The blessing comes when you get to the other side of how devasted you feel. And that does not need to take as long as separation does. To think about separation being years seems long, but once you realize you are a twinflame, what the journey is about, and what your role is, you can find happiness in separation in a short period of time. If you were to follow all the things mentioned in this book, plus or minus any different direction your spirit team steers you, your life will begin to change.

There is nothing you could have done to prevent separation. Twinflames must go through this. We cannot hold ourselves as examples for the collective if we are still wrapped up in the need to get things externally, especially from our twin. The point of separation is to see that we are connected to something greater. You are one with your twin, even if it doesn't appear that way. Sometimes I look at it like my twin, and I have even something more significant than 3D marriage, so why would I need marriage here? Faith is stronger than a piece of paper, and your soul is infinite, whereas this life has a limit on it. You will leave here one day, and unlike 3D married couples who will part until their next lifetime, you instead remain one with your twin, never to separate because they are you.

There's one way to survive separation. You have to connect with your spirit team. There is no other way around this. Even after you've healed, dealt with your ego and mind, and found your purpose and newfound happiness, you will still have bad days. Not as bad as the days in the beginning, when you didn't want to get out of bed. But there will be days you don't feel on your game or completely lit up, and passionate like you do other days. On a scale of 1-10, if not wanting to get out of bed was a very numb 1-2, this will be more like a five. But five will now feel low to you since you are more used to being at a 10. During those level five days, I find that ego will try to creep back in. Ego seriously fights to survive, but you will start to recognize it easier as you go. You'll see it's just more of an annoyance. Ego, in this stage, begs to bring you back to the early days when you wanted to reach out to your twin and find some way to connect. It wants proof that all of this stuff you are going through is for something it can see. There is only one thing that counteracts that—your spirit team.

This is what I strongly urge you to do during separation. Get close to source, your higher self, your spirit guides, the archangels, and even your twin's higher self. Yes, that's right, even your twin's own higher self. At different stages of your journey, if they see you holding back the process, they will visit you to push you along. But, you do not have to wait for their visits. You can sit and ask them anything you want, anytime. If you want things to move along a bit faster, you may want to do this once a week or a couple of times a month. Reserve time to just sit and ask what is on your mind. Get quiet and activate your third eye. Do a third eye activation ceremony if you don't know how to tap into this yet.

Here's a little trick my ego used to do. It would wake up my inner child and lure her into what it wanted. Then it would feed her messages before I could receive them. So, her heart was involved and would pull on my heartstrings by the time they got to me. My inner child has a strong connection to my twin, so the ego used her to try to get me to contact him. I would have to remind her of divine timing and its purpose before I got swept up in the past.

Your spirit team will answer most questions you need answered, usually providing an answer you didn't expect. It may be why your twin is doing what they are doing or they may provide with what your next lesson needs to be so you can upgrade.

They are very invested in this because they want the two of you together. This is your safe space. When you speak to anyone in the 3D about your twin, you may or may not be supported, and it never really feels like anyone understands how important this person is to you. Well, your spirit teams knows. They feel just what you feel and will never discourage you from thinking of your twin or wanting to talk about them. They will never shame you if you have one of those lower days and need to connect with them to see something other than this crappy 3D illusion that keeps getting thrown in your face. Having 6 or 7 of these powerful forces with you is better than anything you could ever have on earth.

Separation is not only an opportunity for healing, but it is also all of the following:

- Getting to know yourself
- Pursuing your dreams with a clear mind because you have the space you wouldn't otherwise if you were with your twin.
- Getting clear on your purpose and living it
- Learning how codependent your previous relationships have been, including with your twinflame
- Learning how to set boundaries
- Moving past suffering
- Forgiving your twin fully
- Finding new mentors that help with spiritual awakening
- Learning about soul contracts. Let me elaborate on this one. Before you reincarnated, you were one soul. Like a catalog, you chose what you wanted your experience on earth to be like. Picture

that a screen was put in front of you, and each option you picked showed a synopsis of what your story would be like on earth. You chose this journey. You chose the difficulty level that you had to meet before union. You chose your guides, your name, and your trauma. Then you sign a contract with the universe before you are released to the holding queue to go to earth. When you get here, you are basically in a video game. Your obstacles in this game are your trauma, ego, mind, the matrix, and other people, including friends and family. And the most important obstacle - separation. You may level up in areas of your life before separation, but during separation is where the game gets interesting. It gets challenging as fuck. Just like a video game, it's not linear. If you fail out of one level, you are back at the beginning of that level, knowing more about how to get through it, repeating until you get it right. The trick to this is to think of your life exactly like this. To look for the next hidden thing that will get you the extra points you need to obtain the tools that will push you through to the next level. If you haven't experienced this yet, wait; you will.

Believe it or not, your twin will go through this eventually. They will have to face the connection between the two of you, their own spiritual awakening and dark night of the soul. They can't escape it; it's written into the contract. Only there is one brutal rule. You can't speak of this contract until both parties are awake in their own spiritual awakening. Every time you try to convince your twin of something that they aren't ready to hear, you go back 3-5 levels in the game. It's not worth it, and they can't hear you anyway. You might be saying, we are one soul, we are meant to be together, and they will hear nothing but manipulation. You lose when you try to control. It has to be divine timing, and it has to be their free will. Compare this to a real-life example. Say you want a car and a dealership is hounding you to look at their cars every day. Are you going to? Or are you going to look at the cars when you feel inspired to?

Another area where separation can be very confusing is social media messages. Let's say you come across a meme that says the following:

If he constantly makes
you feel like you need to
go to a psychic or a tarot reader
to see how he feels about
you, he ain't the one

This message is great for the average girl in the dating world. But it's not for you. Your twin has walked away from you to benefit both of your lives. They aren't telling you that because you have to figure it out for yourself. Before you understand this, social media posts like this will have your head spinning. If you still look outside the twinflame collective for answers regarding your twin, you will get the wrong information and it will take you off your path.

Now, once you are fully awake to what is going on, you scroll past that stuff, knowing they are the one, and this is a faith-based mission that you believe in. I usually feel tempted to comment, "Except for twinflames."

SEPARATION TIPS

Separation Tip #1

Stop looking at their social media. I know – this one is tough. But you know why we want to look? Mind and ego want to stay in control. You think at least if you know what is going on with them, you have some sense of what is happening with the situation, right? WRONG. You know why – that isn't even your real twin. You've seen your twin at a soul level. They revealed themselves to you at some point, right? Their soul. YOUR SOUL. All you see online is a person still programmed by the matrix going through karmic lessons.

But you feel this strong connection with this person, so what do you do instead? You talk to source, your higher self, and your spirit guides. They are all there with you. Maybe you do this during meditation or another form of sitting quietly. Meditation is not effective for me. I will grab my favorite sparkling water and sit on my couch in the dark. Then I either talk through my problems or ask source questions. One time, I asked about my twin. They said, "Give us time; we are walking with him" That's it! Source isn't complicated like the human experience, mind, and ego are. So, I picture him, walking along the beach with his higher self, with his spirit guides, with source...even with my higher self. Unconditional love from a distance is all he wants from me. It's all they are ever going to want. Nothing more...

Separation Tip #2

Let that ego and mind work for you. They are supposed to be here to help you, not control you. Use them to help you achieve what you want in life. If ego and mind tell you that you can't do this thing or live this dream or that your twin needs to heal before anything in life will work out, they control you. See chapter 6 for more regarding ego and mind.

Separation Tip #3

Create something you love just for you. Remodel a room, paint a canvas, or start a hobby that fascinates you and you've always admired. Benefits to creating include improving your mood and brain function, boosting your self-esteem, and alleviating stress and anxiety.

Separation Tip #4

Be careful whom you work with on this journey and do your healing work. See chapter 5 for information on how to be best supported during this journey.

Separation Tip #5

Don't beat yourself up. When you are upgrading your life, you will feel overwhelmed, take a break, have a luxurious bubble bath, and know everything will be fine. The universe has got you. You may have signed up for this ride that you are unsure of, but you're not alone. You also can't screw this up. Think about it this way. Whenever you make a big ask to the universe, it has to maneuver some things around to make that happen for you. It looks for opportunities to get you what you want. But it is going to hear you distinctly. So, if you asked for a healed counterpart that will respect you, it now has to counteract 20, 30, or 40 years of trauma in that person. It will NOT bring you that person at 30% or 50%. You don't want that. You said you didn't want it. So, you aren't screwing anything up by asking for what you deserve. For example, if your counterpart is in the middle of a karmic lesson (seeing someone else, addictions, family issues/control, etc.) and it looks to you like they are never coming back – what if that karmic lesson is precisely what will turn them into the respectful partner you wanted? Do you support the universe in this? It's working for you, not against you. The dark always comes before the light.

So, here's what you do instead. You list all the things you would like to do in life...no matter how outrageous. Plant medicine retreat? Trip to Italy? Write a book? Get a million followers while traveling in a van? Like what? You only have to do this for 15 minutes. I know that it's a stretch for some of you to dedicate that amount of time to yourself. I was there once.

This list may not come to fruition for a couple of years. It took me that long. But when you start fulfilling this list, you will feel different than you ever have. See, you can sit in a room all day and say, 'I need to detach from my Twinflame, but it won't do anything because your subconscious isn't yet being reprogrammed to believe that you can be happy without your twin...so you will continue to obsess and feel worse every day. You need to keep pushing to reprogram those neural pathways. I'm not saying one weekend away will solve everything. Consistency is key. You know how you always wanted consistency from your twin? Well, they were/are mirroring your own inconsistencies. Do extraordinary things for yourself as often as you possibly can. After a while...you realize it's not your twin that makes you happy; it's you. And then your twin will be more drawn to you because THEY no longer feel pressured to make you happy.

CHAPTER FOUR

THE RIGHT WAY TO DO HEALING WORK

Let's just start off being honest about this. No one is excited to do healing work. It may seem as though some are more interested in it than others, but that's not true. Interest is the wrong word. Motivated by pain would be more accurate. Hitting rock bottom pain, to be even more precise. The treacherous pain that comes from losing someone you love romantically; however, you can also feel it by losing a friend, family member, pet, a job, a home, a business, etc. Quite often, a combination of these things will happen. When the universe is nudging you to grow, you may find you lose a job out of nowhere. Things that used to be fun, like an all-inclusive drinking vacation with friends to Mexico, feels empty. Then you start to lose friends. There will be feelings that are hard to explain. It's like you know there is more to life than where you are. You have no idea what, but you start to explore other avenues little by little.

Whatever your route, you somehow get to the point where you realize you need to do some work on yourself, and you need to face your shadows.

Healing will look different for everyone. One thing I can tell you that is absolutely the same for everyone is that talk therapy will not help you heal. It will support you during a rough time, but it's temporary support. I never want to discourage anyone from doing what they feel called to do, but consider the following:

• Trauma cannot be released from your body without a somatic type of therapy with a professional/therapist/facilitator who has training in this

• Therapists often want you to face things we aren't ready to, so you may lie, lie to the therapist, and even to yourself. Or you may not bring up certain subjects out of fear. You could be blocked by ego. Ego can be sneaky in how it goes about wanting you to hold onto something

• If you can't see where the trauma is being held or why, it will be tough to know how it is affecting you in the present. There are other kinds of therapy that are more comforting in bringing out this kind of pain.

When I went through my trauma work, I searched incessantly for a book to tell me what I could expect next. What does each step feel like, and how low will my lows feel? I couldn't find one that I could understand on my level. Experts like Peter Levine write very informative trauma books. The problem is that these books are written in an informative way for other experts or educators to read. They aren't appropriate for someone in their darkest moments, when they truly needed to understand what going into the dark tunnel is going to feel like, when they can't see any light on the other side. And will light ever come? Where is your hope? Something you can refer to, so you would know if what you are feeling is normal? If you are here reading this, you most likely don't want to feel the current pain you are living in or don't want it to control you anymore. There's got to be more to life than this, right? You hear people talking about life purpose, and you can't even relate to that as it feels so far away. Like miles from the tunnel you just entered, the fearful part is that you don't even know how long that tunnel is. You only see darkness. Is it something you can walk through in a month, in six months, a year? The thought of it taking longer than that is crushing. What comes next? What if you lose who you are now? Then what? It feels empty because it's scary. You hope it doesn't take much longer because these are rough feelings you are experiencing. So, now talk therapy and reading books are pretty much out of the question when it comes to trauma.

And no one around you understands because too much of society uses distractions to cover up painful feelings. It is something you can't just bury any more. How come no one else around you is even considering entering the tunnel? It's because you're beyond acting like it's okay to live with it.

What causes this eruption to happen? By that, I mean, what brings you here? We have stress that we can cope with in everyday life, and then we have things that shake us. I'm talking about things that strip you down, naked, standing in the middle of a barren wheat field in the middle of winter. It's so low; there's no place to go but up. How did you get here? And how do you get out of here? And when no one else in your life is feeling the same way, then what? If we have trauma that hasn't been healed, grief and loss can put us in that field. And when you combine the present-day loss with the unhealed trauma, it can feel like life is hard to live. We are most often alone during this time. No one goes there with us. They can't.

Only you can understand your journey and put the pieces together. At the beginning of healing, even just entering spiritual awakening, you should know this isn't really you. The real you, your soul, and your higher self are still very much disguised. The reason why you feel terrible pain just consumes you is that you are disconnected from who you really are. You don't have to identify with this feeling or who you seem to be.

This is a temporary stretch of highway. You do eventually leave the highway altogether and find yourself on a beach or looking off at a beautiful mountain view. It just takes time and work to get there.

Every person has different experiences that brought them the trauma and different experiences affecting them now. Healing steps are just as unique to each person. You need professionals who will help when you can't find the answers, but you also have to spend much time sitting in that pain you most desperately want to run from. There are many different kinds of trauma healers. Some worked for me that maybe wouldn't work for others. It's more about what you are being called to, and my first tip is to let the pain guide you. Read about everything available and where you feel it pulling you; go in that direction. Don't question it; just do it. Yes, you will have to take your focus off how much it costs and put it on how much your healing is worth. I've spent over $10,000 on actual trauma work and another $8000 on spiritual/growth work. But what good is money if you aren't leading a happy life? What good are the material possessions if they only provide a moment of happiness and then you are back to feeling the pain and emptiness again? Money is a barrier until you release your money blocks. Another barrier might be people in your life not understanding why you need to do this. I don't see growth as a hobby or mere interest as some think. I see it as survival and life fulfillment. It should interest everyone, but it simply won't. One of my spiritual friends once told me a story about her and her sister hiking one day. My friend saw an owl lying near their path in dire need of help and she stopped to rescue it. It had drunk water with chemicals from the agricultural fields nearby. She took it to a vet and saved its life. The interesting part of the story is that her sister walked past the owl first. Why didn't her sister see it? That is the more significant part of the equation that we may never find answers to. The fact that you've picked up this book means you see the owl, and that's a very important step. There will be days when the pain feels like a burden, you may feel like a burden to yourself and others, and it may seem like there's no point in life. That's where you need to know at your core, that it isn't a burden; it's an opportunity. Now, what feels very negative will turn into the polar opposite and become positive. If you are unexplainably drawn towards the light, it is because it is already there, but some stuff covers it up. That stuff is a few, maybe several, things you need to explore. Find out why it's there and work to release it. Ignore everything you've been taught by society and go with your intuition. It's telling you something for a reason. Start with any research around trauma, and it will lead you to where you need to go. It will seem slow at first. For example, I started studying narcissism, which led me to CPTSD, then to trauma healing intensives and therapists, and finally, spiritual retreats like plant medicine. The beginning can be just finding out that not all people on this planet have your best interest at heart and can hurt you. It teaches you that the actions of the people who have hurt you are not okay. This is the duality we need to bring the correct people into our lives. The benefit to the coaches who talk about the darkest places on earth and the betrayal you have experienced, is that they also have the answers to healing.

<u>CPTSD</u>

You probably know what PTSD is. You've heard about veterans needing to do work based on what they may have experienced while away on foreign tours, involved in wars and missions that took them to a dark place in their adulthood. But what's the C? The C technically stands for complex, but I almost prefer to think of it as childhood. This trauma occurs from ages 0-to 18 when your caregivers determine so much about your environment and who you will become as an adult. Again, you will think that your childhood was years ago, and what does it have to do with the present day? But it has everything to do with the present day. What happened to you then is now playing out in your life as an adult. One is affecting the other.

Before discussing how it affects your life today, we need to define trauma. There is big T trauma and little t trauma. Big T trauma consists of sexual abuse or physical/violent abuse. This also includes if a child witnessed either of these being done to someone else. The brain doesn't know the difference. It is the same as if it is happening to the observer. Usually, big T trauma is easier to identify, and more commonly therapy is sought out to work through those issues. If not identified and treated, it can get locked away where you can't reach it, and you can't remember it happened. This feels like the more obvious trauma as it is widely recognized as abuse.

Little t trauma expands into so many other happenings, including the following:

- Neglect
- Yelling
- Insults
- Slapping
- Attacks on thinking processes
- Over control of a child's thoughts

- Not allowing emotional expression
- Shaming emotional expression
- Indulging
- Demanding perfection
- Expecting matching religious beliefs
- Bullying
- Giving things to a child then taking them away when they don't perform. I'm not talking about discipline here, but rather when a child doesn't do something that aligns with the parent; however, it would be perfectly acceptable otherwise.
- Expecting a child to be responsible for a parent's wellbeing, otherwise known as enmeshment.

Here are some explained examples of little t trauma. Remember that abuse can be anything done to you as a child that left you feeling sad, shame, or less than.

Example #1

You were often left to entertain yourself, maybe in your room or to watch TV. Parents often use the TV as a babysitter, not realizing the abuse they inflict on their children. Perhaps they worked too often, were consumed with their issues, or didn't realize your needs, so they didn't provide attention to you. This would give you a feeling of being left on the shelf until someone wanted you. This teaches you that you aren't a priority to anyone, so you don't even learn to make yourself a priority. This also shows you that people are inconsistent with attention and love. Not knowing any of this is wrong, you grow up thinking that this is how people are supposed to be and how they are supposed to treat you. It didn't feel good as a child, but you didn't know any better and thought you felt cared for. It makes you unhappy as an adult because you are now awakening to the fact that this is terrible treatment. Your self-worth is low because you've been taught you are low priority. This is the first example of the shadow they refer to in shadow work.

Example #2

Your parents dragged you to church every week. Something inside you hated going to church. To make your parents happy, you tried to enjoy the hymns at least and did your best to keep your mind off the preacher telling you how bad you are. On top of that, people in the church seem fake and hypocritical. They are not as wonderful as they make themselves out to be. You express to your parents that you no longer wish to attend church, and not only are you shamed for this want but you are forced to continue to go. You may have even been part of a

THE RIGHT WAY TO DO HEALING WORK

family where you had to do more than Sunday morning church, like outside catholic classes or Mormon missions. If they are not things you want to be doing, these things can be horrific. You do what your parents tell you. Again, you don't know if you can say no or aren't being provided a choice. This can also come through in other areas, for example:

• You want to be an artist, but your parents insist you be a doctor or a lawyer
• You want to date, but your parents decide whom you can and can't date or, even worse, arrange a marriage for you
• You are gay or trans, but your parents threaten to disown you if you don't change to be straight. You may have even been sent to a group or camp to change your mind
• You are shamed for how you want to dress, cut your hair, or even what you weigh

Your wants and desires are supposed to be acknowledged as a child, but many parents believe that children are born to follow in their footsteps. Some parents will go as far as trying to recreate their lives through their children. As a unique soul, you were born with specific traits and desires and will most times conflict with what your parents want for you. This again becomes a shadow that causes you pain because you are now used to creating your life around others' wants, not your own. On top of that, your soul is not fulfilled, and this becomes crushing to you as an individual. At some point, you will feel a stronger desire to say no as your soul's desire becomes louder.

Example #3

You are bullied at school by other kids. No one sticks up for you, you may be left to eat lunch by yourself, or you find it hard to make friends because the bullies spread rumors about you, causing your entire grade to look at you as less than. This one will most definitely cause shame and low self-worth, but it will also have severe consequences on how you connect with others. You may be willing to connect with anyone, even if they are not serving you, rather than be selective about whom you let into your life. Does it make sense how trauma translates to shadows?

We often don't think about these things or dismiss them as normal. It was all you knew and may have assumed that everyone went through it, so normal should mean it didn't affect you, right? Wrong. It did. There is no perfect parent in the world. We celebrate Mother's Day and Father's Day and buy our parents gifts that say Best Dad or Most Wonderful mother. These people are still human, though, and they made mistakes. Whether they meant to make them or not isn't the issue, and this is again where you may feel alone on your journey.

As we start to uncover the different areas where this can affect you, you may want your parents or caregivers to make it better, but most of the time, they won't. It's normal and what's most important to remember is that this is about you. This book is entirely about you. If you were neglected or told you were wrong, this is the first day you get to change that because every human on this planet has a good heart buried underneath their pain. When you go through trauma work, you will cry more tears than you thought you had. This is precisely what is supposed to happen. I want you to think back to when you were a little boy or girl. I want you to think of a time when you were full of light and happy, or you had a smile that was so strong that you felt playful and joyful. Now think of a time when something happened that stole that light and your smile. Was it something someone said or someone leaving you? Don't think of just parents; think of teachers, siblings, family friends or bullies, anyone in your life that could have possibly changed a moment where you were feeling fine, then suddenly sad or confused. Every time something like this happened, your inner child was hurt. And I'm going to tell you something that may bring that first tear. You did not deserve it. Repeat that to yourself a few times or as often as you need to.

Trauma can begin to occur as early as the time you are in the womb and can occur as late as moments ago. The way we handle negative events as an adult is a result of our childhood trauma. When trauma happens to you as a child, you create coping mechanisms to deal with it. There is an instinct within humans to survive. If you were to fully feel what happened to you as a child, it might've caused damage in irreparable ways or risked your survival. As you live through anything from neglect to sexual or violent abuse, you were still a child that was dependent upon others. You needed to please your caregivers to get fed, have shelter over your head, and receive love. This may be the first time you've ever thought about this, so let it sink in. Your survival was entirely dependent upon others and out of your control. This made you helpless and defenseless. You didn't have a choice as you do today to move away or stop talking to people if they don't treat you right. The conditions and experiences you had were not out of choice. It is valuable to make a list of those experiences. Think of everything that disappointed you, hurt you, and anyone who disrespected you. Then list how it made you feel beside it. Write in a third spot how you wished it had been instead.

Now name what each one is. Is it neglect? Abandonment? Abuse? And then, I want you to read back over your desired results. Your wish lists. This is actually what you deserved and what should have happened. When you go through trauma healing with a professional healer, they will often ask you to send that pain back to the person who gave it to you. It's very important to energetically return it to them. It doesn't belong with you. It never did.

You may feel like you are betraying your parents or siblings or caregivers or teachers, or others. This is not actually about blame. Whether your parents are the best or the worst or where they fall compared with other parents is not the point of this work. We are not blaming or defining them. We simply note that you did not deserve to be treated this way. No little boy or little girl does. This is all about you. You aren't playing victim to do this exercise. You are entitled to do work that will allow you to release your past.

As you read more about CPTSD and start to gain knowledge, you will learn how it has affected you and played out in your life. This is where you need skilled trauma therapists to do some of the heavy lifting with you.

For example, here are some of the ways trauma affected my life:

o I wanted to fix emotionally unavailable men to cure my feeling of wanting to save my dad

o I didn't pursue hobbies or passions because I had a belief that they didn't matter. I was just here to work and cope with vices like TV and alcohol

o I didn't take good care of myself through fitness as this wasn't done in my family, and I felt like I didn't deserve that. It was something other people did

o I became a doormat, more concerned with pleasing others than myself, with everyone from boyfriends to the person driving behind me on the freeway

o I threw things when I was furious – just like my mother

None of these things are who I am. None of the items on your list are who you are either. Moreover, they are things you started doing to survive and 'fit in' or things that you were made to believe about yourself. Healing and finding yourself is a reset. You are allowed to decide what is and isn't you and change anything and everything if you want to.

Your dedication to this process is vital. I don't say that to scare you. Have patience, and don't give up hope. I promise the answers are there. They will take time, and I hope this book will help to guide you toward them. Once you start finding the resources and get involved with them, you will eventually be led to other ones. You are unique, so just like I said that your trauma is unique, your healing is too. Find one thing from this book that draws you in and go with it. It will most definitely lead you to the next one. And then the next one. And they finally lead to a place where the pain feels like an actual memory. You aren't alone.

TRAUMA AND LOVE

Being in a relationship should feel like two warm hands holding each other with compassion and tenderness. The triggering that comes with Twinflames can feel like those same two hands were shaped into fists that smacked up against each other. They tend to cause immense amounts of pain. My twinflame once said, "I don't believe I am a bad person." And he's right; he's not. However, the hurt he felt as a little boy had been dragged into his life as an adult and was now affecting everyone who tried to love him. Our relationship gave me an in-depth experience regarding attachment styles.

There are 4 or 5 attachment styles; however, I am only going to discuss 3 of them for this book.

Secure Attachment

Secure attachment is what we should all strive to be. Secure people don't take things personally in relationships, don't play games, and are usually fairly consistent in providing attention and keeping boundaries. They aren't attached to anyone in an unhealthy way and don't fear love.

You only become automatically secure if your caregivers rarely neglected you and gave you attention when you wanted it and never when you didn't. They didn't force feelings upon you that were theirs and allowed you to express yours. They also would have encouraged you to set your own boundaries when appropriate.

Anxious Attachment

Anxious Attachment style is what some might call the needy or clingy type. If you are anxiously attached, you probably had a parent who was not always available to you or for you as a child. This caused an abandonment wound that carries into adult life. Even though you are now safe as an adult, the trauma of not having your needs met when you were little affects your adult relationships. It makes you believe anyone in your life will abandon you.

Avoidant Attachment

Avoidant attachments are those who put up walls or push their partner away. They most likely grew up with parents who were often dismissive or punishing of their emotions, which taught them that vulnerability is unsafe and emotions should be kept quiet. This leaves the child with no choice but to stuff them down. Most of our divine masculines are dealing with this kind of attachment issue. It takes them longer to seek help because it is challenging for this kind of person to open up or seek help from anyone. They were taught not to. I've personally heard my twin say that he doesn't believe he should have to pay someone for help and tries to write off therapy as a cult. It's fairly common that divine masculines view the work in this way. Completely acceptable that they grow in the gym or at work, but growing in any way that involves vulnerability seems out of the question.

And yes, you may be a combination of all three at times, but you typically carry one more than the others. As humans, we are all the same. We long for companionship, and love runs through our veins, but when two people with trauma get involved, the teachings from childhood, locked away in the unconscious, come out to play.

If you are not familiar with our brains' conscious and unconscious parts, let me explain further. Do you know how you drive home and often forget how you got there? That is your unconscious brain in action. There's nothing wrong with that. It is part of being human.

When you are learning something new, like driving for the first time, you are using your conscious brain. Another example is when you start a new job and have to learn everything from the beginning, your brain starts to feel tired and spins. That is because you spent the whole day at this job using your conscious brain.

The conscious brain uses up a ton of energy. Think of it like it is the expensive part to run. You only have so much cash, so you can only use it for so long. And once the money runs out, you can't access it anymore. That is your conscious brain doing its job and then needing to rest. If we had to use our conscious brain all day, every day, we wouldn't be able to function as humans. There is just no way to have enough energy to feed it. This is why the unconscious brain was created. It runs much cheaper. When you learn something through the conscious, and you've got it down, it gets stored in the unconscious where it can repeat the pattern over and over again quickly. So, driving home doesn't require much attention once you've done it a few times. You are on autopilot, and your conscious brain is reserved for when you genuinely need it.

Biologically this serves you. When it comes to trauma and abuse, it does not. If someone told you that you were worthless ten times and you never heard that you were worthy, the worthlessness gets stored in your subconscious. You don't even realize it's happening. Just like you were never really cognizant of driving home, you would not be aware that you don't think you are worthy. You would go along in everyday life thinking you love yourself. It's hard to see the unconscious script running the 'I am unworthy; I am unworthy' track. You then act it out without knowing. Others can see that you aren't valuing yourself, but you won't until someone hurts you.

Often, when your unconscious actions begin hurting you and your life, you end up meeting with a coach or therapist. When the time comes for them to address the low self-esteem, you may still be in denial about it. It's hard to understand at first that you not loving yourself is unhealed abuse and trauma. It's pretty common for people who haven't done their childhood trauma work to feel retraumatized by this shame because you think it's your fault. It takes a long time to realize you didn't do this to yourself. You do have to recover from it, but you didn't wake up one day and decide to allow others to hurt you. You were taught it was acceptable. This is NOT your fault and is why it is imperative to do somatic therapy to release trauma from your body first and then also to feel the compassion of that healer. For some, this kind of therapy is sometimes the first time a person feels this sort of kindness and concern from another human being. When parents or caregivers never provided this to you when you were little, you often don't know it exists, and you don't know to ask your partner for it, nor do they know to give it to you since they are your mirror and just as ill-equipped. To be crying and have a professional there with one-on-one attention to help you let those feelings come out is something every human should experience and have access to at some point in their lives. Those who grew up feeling unworthy and pick the partners who reflect them usually only know how to get close to someone through sex. They may think that this is them being intimate, but it is not. You can have sex without being vulnerable, but somatic trauma release requires openness. It wakes you up to being vulnerable in a way you have never been before, and the healer you are working with helps you feel safe so you can let it happen. It is powerful to see another person care for you in this way when there isn't sex at all involved. So many people are just jumping into sex on the first, third, or fifth date. Because #1 is the only closeness they know #2 they believe they are unworthy of having that other person around unless they can offer their body and sexual gratification. Imagine if a person just wanted to sit under the stars and talk to you about the beauty of the universe or if they were willing to hold you for 20-30 minutes while you cried. You may want this, most people do, but do you feel worthy of it?

Back to the brain. Working with healers will change your unconscious programming. Note: saying this and experiencing it are two different things. If you haven't lived this, you cannot believe it. Second, you then practice affirmations, gratitude, meditation, etc. This all, little by little, starts reprogramming those parts of your unconscious. The 'I am unworthy' will be replaced by 'I am worthy.' Have grace and patience with yourself. If you are 20, 30, or 40 years old, you went through ALL those years of the wrong programming. It will take a while to shift into the new you.

The more you do this, the easier it is for the

conscious brain to step in a little more and help you. For example, if you are approached by someone seeking to take advantage of you, it will be easier for you to see the red flags. The conscious will be able to alert you more that you've seen something like this before and direct you to walk away.

Sometimes you have to spend more time alone and reject people in your life until you've done the work to attract the right ones. It may seem challenging to do so. There will be days and nights where you think, why'd I give all those people up? They're all I have. It's a risk. And it feels like a risk of betraying yourself and betraying the people you believe you love. But you need to think about it this way: your life of trauma brought these people to you. And on the healing path, those people will no longer fit. They won't understand. If you try to talk to them about it, your experiences won't make any sense to them. I've found I get more aggravated trying to explain what's happening inside me, and it never really lands for them anyway. Time is better spent surrounding yourself with people who are doing the work or listening to ones that have. With the experts that are there as the pain comes up. Also, these people won't be around enough; they never can be. That's where you start to find the strength in yourself. To survive on this planet, we truly only need ourselves. Society has taught you to depend on others, but if you do, you will be led by how they lead their lives and their limitations as well. Look at someone close to you. Is there something that you bond over? Do you have a hard time setting boundaries with them? Do you never feel appreciated? A situation with limiting beliefs can often override your own goals and desires. You've bonded with this person over these agreements. When you work on healing, you break these ties to them. It's a choice, but you've chosen to see things differently. Now you see the owl on the path, and you can't live with not making it better. You are driven to make it different, to make the pain subside. You are now in the unknown. Nothing is certain at all. Because you have to start over with many things and recreate yourself.

There are a lot of different feelings wound up in pain itself. In this chapter, I will explain various modalities for releasing trauma. Through any of these, you will get into your body and identify where pain is stored. Is it held in the chest? In the gut? Is it hard to breathe? Does it feel tight? This is all trauma. It has had nowhere to go, so it sits and causes physical pain, sometimes disease, and even cancer. Trauma can keep you in states of fight, flight, freeze, or fawn. Fight occurs when the nervous system feels it needs to face a perceived threat aggressively. Flight occurs when needing to run from a threat. Freeze is being unable to move or act against the threat. Fawn is acting to please in order to avoid conflict. The first two are helpful if you are about to encounter a snake or puma on your hiking path, but they are unnecessary for everyday life. Trauma has turned them into an 'on' position for many waking days and sleepless nights. What trauma work does is help to turn those off. Your logical brain may know to keep them turned off, but your unconscious brain does not, and the unconscious is in charge most of the time. Reprogramming is required. Freeze used to show up for me all the time when someone would want something I didn't. My throat chakra was shut down and I could gain the strength to exercise my boundaries.

Trauma Healing Intensives

Intensives are sessions working with some of the world's most professional and powerful healers. This is not your average therapy and is the real deal in the world of healing work. Intensives typically last five days or a week, and you work in small groups, or one on one with a trauma therapist. This is a safe space to explore and release the trauma.

I've listed some resources at the end of this

chapter. If you want to know more about a real-life experience of someone working through their childhood trauma, you can read Neil Strauss's book, The Truth. This is the same book I talk about in Chapter 10 in regards to the divine masculine.

In reading this book, I was called to do work at the same place Neil Strauss went to. At The Meadows, I wrote out my childhood trauma, I cried it out and released it through a window with a highly experienced trauma therapist right beside me. Then I did chair work to remove my shame and see how my inner child was leading my life. Typically, they introduce you to your inner child and allow them to express their pain by imagining one of your parents coming into the room and letting them say all they want to say. They tailor this entire experience to what you need. Many believe that children aren't cognizant in life until they start walking and talking, but it is now known that trauma can start registering in a human as early as in the womb.

EMDR & Brainspotting, Somatic Experiencing and Completion Therapy

The methods work differently than talk therapy. They target stored trauma and get it released. You may release this through crying, screaming, laughing or shaking. Professionals help you locate the source of the trauma and discharge it for good.

See explanations for all three of these healing methods in the healing resources at the end of this chapter.

Plant Medicine

There are many plant medicines you can research to see what might work best for you. Plant medicines have been used for thousands and thousands of years. Similar to the healing methods mentioned above, plant medicine works with releasing trauma. It is a much faster, more effective way of tackling trauma and any other issues you may have in your life. It is helpful to set intentions with plant medicine, but the plant knows what you need. Once you ingest it, you will be guided through a personalized experience unique to you. The only reason they are not widely used today amongst the collective is because systems were created to push them underground. Big pharma won't be able to keep making their profits if every city has psychedelics available legally. We would be a healed, peaceful population if that were the case. There are still people today in the Amazon that only use plants for healing. They probably don't even know what the word pharmacy means. To them, the jungle is their 'pharmacy.'

The most popular medicines are Ayahuasca, Psilocybin, peyote, iboga, MDMA (ecstasy), and ketamine.

Please only do these with skilled healers and do your research before choosing who to work with. The healers I worked with in Costa Rica were required to do extensive training, including spending a year alone in the jungle, becoming one with the plants and the medicine. This is incredibly important as your trauma will be released from your crown chakra, and you need to be in a safe, supportive container. It has been said plant medicine is often compared to doing 5-10 years of therapy in one week, and I can concur. It starts integrating you even before you go to the retreat and will work with you for a long time after you return home.

This medicine helped me release any remaining trauma I had in my body. You can see my experience with Ayahuasca on my YouTube channel at breakingloveopen. You can also refer to the recommendations at the end of this chapter for other videos explaining Ayahuasca and its benefits.

At Home Healing Work

If you cannot afford the above methods right now, I recommend financing them. It will be worth it. This kind of treatment changes your entire life. If you aren't ready for that, then release your trauma on your own. Sit with your feelings every chance you get. Ask where in the body am I feeling this? Allow it to process and then pass through your heart chakra, and that particular feeling will never be seen again. You will experience feelings that may *feel* the same, but every distinct one that passes through is more trauma gone. Ask what this is? A lot of this will be childhood-related. Try to see if you can relate to a time in life when you were younger and felt the same as you do now. For example, in separation from your twin, do you feel the same way as when a parent abandoned you early in life? When was the first time you felt that way? How old were you? Feel it. The more you cry, the more you punch pillows, or scream into a towel, the more you release. Don't stay here, however. There is no need to. Once you pass it through the heart chakra, you train your mind that you don't always have to stay stuck here. You can move on from trauma and despite what you may hear, healing is not a lifelong event.

Coping Mechanisms

Here's another free one and one that everyone must do. It's coping mechanisms. Yep, sorry. I need you to sit down and list everything that is aiding you in escaping from life. What is stopping you from feeling your feelings? What is stopping you from progressing forward? Alcohol? Smoking? Codependency with family or friends? Shopping? Weed? Porn? Work? Whatever you have written down slowly needs to be weaned out. Don't try cold turkey; it won't work. Let's take alcohol, for example. Pick a week, any week – this time, you will go to the grocery store and not bring home that wine or tequila or whatever your weakness is. It's just a week. If your mind overrides you and you visit the store later and have a glass of wine in your hand out of nowhere, drink the wine with no shame. The ego will try to make you feel like shit at this point. Allow it to be there. Allow it to pass. Then when you are ready, you take another trip to the grocery store without buying alcohol.

Eventually, you become more conscious about your actions and how they affect you. Enough times, you get to a point where you don't even want it. I drink wine now, and all I taste is carcinogens and the after-effect of a headache. In time, one after another, the coping mechanisms go, and you will see clearly what they were doing to you. Nothing changes without a starting point.

Boundaries
I highly recommend taking a workshop on

boundaries. In a nutshell, you need to practice saying no and speaking up for yourself. And then you need to sit with that boundary forever. For example, let's say that you get back in touch with your twinflame and they want to see you one evening. Your friends have decided that they all want to go drinking that night and want you to come. Your inner voice tells you that you need time alone with your twin. The people-pleaser inside of you says that time alone with your twin doesn't matter and that you should take this opportunity to introduce your twin to all your friends. You say no to the friend stating that you want to be alone with him because you haven't had any time with him in so long, and your relationship with him is delicate right now. The friend says, 'You can spend the rest of the weekend with him, come on, we really want you there and we want to meet him too.' Your inner voice tries to beckon you again, but the people pleaser in you wins, you go out for the evening, and it puts you and your twin in a fight because what you both needed was time alone. You weren't happy, and your twin wasn't either. Why did you say yes again? Because you didn't know how to set a boundary with this person.

Let's examine how this should have gone. Let's say that you get back in touch with your twinflame and they want to see you one evening. Your friends have decided that they all want to go drinking that night and want you to come. Your inner voice says, 'You need time alone with your twin; it's important.' You say no to the friend organizing the evening, and you tell her to have fun at the event. You don't tell her about your plans or whom you plan to spend them with. You simply say you are busy.

This doesn't give this person an in to change your mind because you didn't provide details that they can use against you to change your mind. If they try anyway, by saying something like 'Why not?', you simply repeat yourself or even ignore the person. If you further explain or defend yourself for any reason, you have now given this person permission to question you even more in an attempt to change your mind. It will feel uncomfortable to say no again or to walk away after the second no, but you must sit with the uncomfortable feeling and understand that your needs matter. Your wants and desires matter, and you are not living this life to cave to others. You don't owe others any explanation why you do or don't want to do something. This doesn't mean any of this has to be rude or hurtful. It just is. Again, you were conditioned as a child not to say no. Parents hate that word, right? You hear it all the time. So now, you have to reset that unconscious training and retrain yourself so that you can say no whenever you damn well please and don't need to explain why. Not having boundaries is a form of people-pleasing that will rob you of your life.

Codependency

This is another one I would recommend an online workshop for. You MUST master codependency to be back in union. I talk about codependency throughout this book, but it would be good to do a workshop where you are provided exercises to see how this is showing up in your life. The way this showed up for me, was me talking someone's ear off until I got their approval and validation. I couldn't stand being alone and sometimes accepted company from people I didn't want to be around. You may also see this playing out in your life as accepting bad behavior from others and finding yourself putting up with unsolicited advice from people who don't even have their own lives together.

In chapter 8, I talk about being alone and finding yourself and the magic that can create in your life. Codependency deprives you of that magic because all you are doing is living someone else's magic. It can't continue because it is dependent on the other person to provide it. To be clear, the 'magic' you feel *with* another person will never compare to your own. Similar, maybe, but your own magic will fulfill you and excite you in a way that codependency never will. Codependency is the #1 reason that twinflames are apart. They need freedom within in order to come together.

Inner Child

Your inner child of all ages lives in your adult body today. Even after doing trauma work, you will still need to acknowledge and engage with your inner child. This will be hard for some at first. Here are some tips:

- Get a picture of you as a little boy or girl and keep it by your nightstand. Look at this child you see and love them for everything they are. There are no imperfections in this child. See how precious they are. They are loved, greatly…by you.
- Allow your inner child to write you a letter of whatever they feel they need to express to you. Write it with your non-dominant hand to appear like a child is writing it. This will help you to step into your inner child's thoughts. This has been bottled up inside you for a long time. It's time for it to

come out.

• In adult form, write them back with your dominant hand, and respond to their concerns, wants, or desires. Respond how you wish you had been responded to when you were little. Tell them they are loved.

• Show them around your new life. Wounded inner children often feel unsafe. If something in your environment made you feel unsafe when you were little, your inner child still feels that way today. Show them that they are now protected. They are with you and no longer in the old environment, nor do they ever have to return there.

• Do activities with them. Paint, color, watch a kid's movie or take them to the park. What do you wish you had done more of as a kid? Do that and rewrite your childhood.

• Hug them. If hugging is too much at first, can you hold their hand? If this is too hard to do yourself, see if you can book a session with a trauma therapist who will sit with you as you cry out whatever pain you are still holding onto. This is a very powerful healing process to connect with your inner child. They need to be acknowledged and loved.

- As you move through your life, start acknowledging if actions are being made by your unhealed inner child or you as an adult. You are the parent at this point. Your inner child may want to eat ice cream all day, but you know better. I'm not saying you can't ever indulge in having a bowl of ice cream with your inner child, but reparenting is learning and enforcing these limits. You must step fully into the parent role and not let your inner child lead the way.

Think about it this way. Your caregivers made mistakes. Acted out of their trauma. They weren't focused enough or didn't know enough to raise you in a way that would allow you to have a healthier, more successful, less painful life. So now you have to do this for yourself. The little boy or girl you grew up as is still with you today, living inside you and helping you make choices every day through your unconscious mind. In ways, you don't even realize. So, to reset the neural pathways fixed for you by your influencers growing up, you must become the parent and use relationships with your new coaches and experts to teach you a new way. And it has to be the right ones. If you don't have the right people teaching how to reprogram, you risk the little boy or girl inside not understanding the changes occurring, and they will want to pull you back to what both of you know. Another challenge comes up when the ego and the inner child tend to team up with one another. Neither likes change because they both fear it. Keep them as separate as possible by being consistent with your inner child work.

You will know when it's time connect with him/her, if you are:

- o Being reactive
- o Acting overly emotional
- o Trying to fix others
- o People pleasing and approval seeking
- o Feeling lonely
- o Feeling negative self-worth
- o Feeling defensive
- o Always having to be right
- o Fearing abandonment
- o Allowing unhealthy boundaries

Reparenting can show up in really simple ways. Like when you were little and told you couldn't have the cookie before dinner, it's the same now. You are resetting the rules. This may be a bad habit or an addiction. For example, falling asleep to TV is a perfect example of a coping mechanism. A person may evolve this habit because they need a distraction from pain or anxiety. And reparenting might take them to a sleep psychologist to learn how to sleep without it. Sex, drugs, alcohol, shopping, gambling, etc., are examples of a person hiding from pain in the best way they know-how. But there's no need to react based on the feeling of pain. You heal it, you release it, and you will begin to think about your decisions and make better ones as you go through your journey. You will be able to reflect on why those decisions were made in the first place and begin to forgive yourself and others, knowing that none of you knew better. It seems far away. You wish reading this one book would be all the work you have to do. We all wish it were that easy. Reparenting takes time. Enjoy the journey as you carry out each new step and begin to master it. This time you are going to learn how to do it right. The harder you work at it, and the more discipline you provide for yourself and your inner child, the faster it goes. Your inner child needs to feel safe with you, above all else. Be the new parent. Allow your mentors to show you parenting if you can't because you're just not ready for it. They will be strict with you to teach you to be tough with yourself. I have met too many people along my journey who said they had been doing the work for years, and yet nothing had changed. I believe that they allowed too many excuses to stop themselves from forming new behaviors. Going to therapy or trauma intensives is step one. Nothing happens without fully signing on to change. When you are healing, you will make better progress if you aren't surrounded by others who will hold you back. There comes a time when you only want to be around people who will lift you into higher vibration levels, and you want to do the same for them. The friends that think this is inappropriate aren't ready and shouldn't be influencing any part of your life. It is necessary to understand that not everyone is on your path right now, and that's okay because if it comes down to it, you are all you need.

RESOURCES FOR HEALING

TRAUMA-HEALING THERAPIES

- **Eye Movement Desensitization and Reprocessing (EMDR)**
  - EMDR (Eye Movement Desensitization and Reprocessing) is a psychotherapy that enables people to heal from the symptoms and emotional distress resulting from disturbing life experiences. Repeated studies show that by using EMDR therapy, people can experience the benefits of psychotherapy that once took years to make a difference. It is widely assumed that severe emotional pain requires a long time to heal. EMDR therapy shows that the mind can, in fact, heal from psychological trauma much as the body recovers from physical trauma. When you cut your hand, your body works to close the wound. If a foreign object or repeated injury irritates the wound,

it festers and causes pain. Once the block is removed, healing resumes. EMDR therapy demonstrates that a similar sequence of events occurs with mental processes. The brain's information processing system naturally moves toward mental health. If the system is blocked or imbalanced by the impact of a disturbing event, the emotional wound festers and can cause intense suffering. Once the block is removed, healing resumes. Using the detailed protocols and procedures learned in EMDR therapy training sessions, clinicians help clients activate their natural healing processes.

Find a practitioner: emdr.com, then EMDR Info

- **Somatic Experiencing**
  - Somatic Experiencing (SE™) is a body-oriented therapeutic model applied in multiple professions and professional settings—

psychotherapy, medicine, coaching, teaching, and physical therapy — for healing trauma and other stress disorders. It is based on a multidisciplinary intersection of physiology, psychology, ethology, biology, neuroscience, indigenous healing practices, and medical biophysics and has been clinically applied for more than four decades. It is the life's work of Dr. Peter A. Levine. The SE approach releases traumatic shock, which is key to transforming PTSD and the wounds of emotional and early developmental attachment trauma. It offers a framework to assess where a person is "stuck" in the fight, flight, or freeze responses and provides clinical tools to resolve these fixated physiological states. SE provides effective skills appropriate to a variety of healing professions, including mental health, medicine, physical and occupational therapies, bodywork, addiction treatment, first response, education, and others.

Find a practitioner: directory.traumahealing.org

- **Brainspotting**
  - Brainspotting therapy works for everyone. Brainspotting gives the therapist access to both the brain and body. The goal is to bypass the conscious thinking processes of the neo-cortex to get to the deeper, more emotional, and body-based processes from the sub-cortex part of the brain. Brainspotting can be the primary mode of treatment, or it can be integrated with the expertise already being provided.

    Find a practitioner: brainspotting.com, then BSP Directory

- **Completion Process by Teal Swan**
  - The Completion Process is a comprehensive approach to healing. It is an 18-step visualization that walks you through an emotional

trigger, following the emotion to the earliest memory, then resolving the child's needs through both the mental visualization of resolution and providing awareness through the adult perspective of the events that occurred.

Find a Practioner: competitionprocess.com, then Practitioners.

INTENSIVES FOR INDIVIDUALS

- **Breaking Free** OR **Facing the Shadow at Pine Grove**
Pinegrovetreatment.com
- **Childhood Trauma Workshop at The Meadows**
themeadows.com, then Mental Health, then Trauma. There is a section just for Childhood Trauma
- **Ayahuasca Plant Medicine:** retreatguru.com, then search for Ayahuasca
- **Soltara Ayahuasca Retreats:** Website: soltara.co

• **Maegical Healing Ayahuasca & Psilocybin Retreats** – If you attend the retreat with Psilocybin, it will reprogram your limiting beliefs. This is one I plan to do in the future when they offer individual retreats just for this purpose, as I've already done enough with Ayahuasca. Website: maegical.com

Ayahuasca Experiences on YouTube: Breakingloveopen – I have two videos. One explaining the retreat I went to and one with my experience Spiritverse: The Secret Mysteries of Ayahuasca.

ONLINE COURSES

• **Boundary Work:** Create the Love by Mark Groves, Become a Boundaries Badass Createthelove.com

• **Codependency Work:** Create the Love by Mark Groves, Crushing Codependency

Createthelove.com

<u>CHAPTER FIVE</u>

DO YOU NEED A TWINFLAME COACH?

I always thought there was something wrong with me growing up. I would be sitting at a dinner table on Thanksgiving Day, and relatives that I only see once or twice a year would ask me questions about my life. I would feel uncertain about how to answer them. I automatically looked at one of my parents for guidance or maybe to even wanted them to answer for me. I did this late into my thirties, perhaps even looking at my best friend across the table if we were sitting with a group of friends or co-workers and being questioned the same way. Then the person who asked the question would say, 'What are you looking at them for?' I don't know, why was I looking at them? It was a question about me! Shouldn't I know the answer? Shouldn't I know myself well enough to say exactly how I feel about something or what I want from my life? No, I didn't. In my life, I wasn't given the freedom to choose. I didn't know there were options. Everything was just decided for me, and when people asked me otherwise, it was a whole new experience. This was how badly I depended upon the external and not knowing or even hearing my inner voice.

It didn't help that I was an only child and kept to myself. However, I suspect most children suffer some form of this. Most parents don't create environments where their children thrive based of their own wants and desires.

Even as an adult, people continue to provide unsolicited advice and the cycle continues. Everyone who hasn't put their ego in check allows it to control the conversation without the conscious knowing that they should ask someone first if they even want advice. On top of that, social media and the internet are full of information telling us how to think, live, and what to do next. Especially as a divine feminine, when we start having issues with our counterpart or go into separation, we automatically feel as though we need advice and support with this too. You may have been in therapy before you knew you were a twinflame. Then you find out you are on this journey, and it's not like you can speak to just anyone about this. Everyone is full of judgment, sometimes even those that claim they are twinflames but have conflicting information from what you are feeling.

This journey can seem horrible, complex, and challenging. It is natural, after all that, to want to reach out and book an appointment with the first twinflame coach you come across, especially when you have spent most of your life depending on information and advice from others.

Since the Twinflame Journey, however, is a

spiritual mission, it is about your soul. That makes it a very exclusive and personal experience. Your separation time will be different compared to others; your trauma will differ, and your experiences and perception of life will be just as unique as your mission. Even what you need to come into union is going to be different.

What are you expecting when you make that $111 appointment for twinflame coaching? Answers, right? Except you will probably come away feeling possibly more confused than when you started the session. You may get a small aha moment. They may have passed along a tidbit of insight that applied to your situation, but you often feel you didn't get what you paid for. Why? Well, that's because they don't know you as you know you. Unless they are a highly trusted intuitive, they also won't know your spirit guides or be able to access any of the archangels you can access yourself. If you find an intuitive that seems never to steer you wrong, then continue with them, but I would still be cautious on how often you meet with them. Their goal should be to help you start the process and let you go, not keep you coming to them for advice forever.

Regular coaches are going to teach you what they learned on their journey. They are speaking only from what they know. Here are some examples of my experiences to help make sense of this:

Twinflame Coach #1

The first month I found out I was a twinflame, I purchased an online book and was so impressed with the amount of new information this eBook contained that I jumped at booking a session with the author. Her primary directive was that my healing would also directly heal my twinflame and that I was to send him tremendous amounts of love. I did this whenever I could over the next two weeks. I felt incredibly empowered by my role in this and consumed myself with channeling deep into my divine masculine's reality while sending him healing and love. I would display a picture of him on my phone while working and send him all my energy.

Two nights while doing his healing work, I felt more significant amounts of pain than I had ever felt during my own healing. I would cry for hours, and I felt so much despair. I could also feel a very dark cloud swirling around me. It appeared like a hurricane. I had never experienced anything like this in my life. It was so horrible that I messaged this twinflame coach and described what I was experiencing. At first, she backed her advice, and when I explained even more how dark this experience was, she simply stated he must be a karmic connection and said she could refer me to someone who could help me cut that cord.

Twinflame Coach #2

I did not ever sign up with the coach I am about to tell you about, but this example will show you better why coaching doesn't work most of the time and how it can even delay your union.

There is a twinflame coach online whose main philosophy is that we are the soul, not the mind, and not the ego. He stresses this fact over and over again, and if you ask him any personal questions about your journey, he will likely repeat that to you once again. He claims that healing work is unnecessary and that you do not need to acknowledge your inner child. He states that once he read the Power of Now and The Untethered Soul and logically understood his soul connection, he was all better, and his twinflame returned. He uses the fact that they are still in union today as his selling point. Where it gets interesting is that he states his twinflame rejects the ideas of twinflames altogether. She does not acknowledge the twinflame journey, and your twinflame won't either. He says if you watch his videos and purchase his online course for around $400-700, your twin will unblock you or contact you. He has videos about successful unions that he claims happened right after the divine feminine took his course or watched his videos.

Now, I am not doubting part of his story. Most men have an easier time learning something logical. Women typically do not. This is why there are books written about us being from different planets. Women have a flow of emotions that are up one day and down the next. We can be happy one minute, and a movie could have us in tears an hour later. We are the waves, while the men are more the still calm. They are logical when we are not.

This is a pretty forgotten concept regarding spirituality and Twinflame awakening because everything gets assigned masculine or feminine energy, and that's where the focus remains. While I agree these energies are vital in this journey, I think it is essential to remember that men and women have core differences outside of the masculine/feminine arena.

I also strongly disagree that healing and inner child work isn't required. No book or online course can replace the human touch and closeness of the traumatic release therapies I described in chapter 4. In fact, I would not recommend reading The Power of Now or the Untethered Soul until after a certain amount of trauma work has been done. I do not believe we need to do healing work for longer than 1-

3 years if the focus is there. It may need to be revisited from time to time, and it is helpful if you already know how to handle a trigger or how to speak to your inner child to calm them down at a moment's notice. Another point I will disagree with is him stating your counterpart will not go through a spiritual awakening or acknowledge the twinflame journey. This again may be true for his journey, but I don't believe that is the way the universe intended it. I believe he is spiritually bypassing and never did the work involved, nor gave his counterpart the time to spiritually awaken. If she is still asleep, there is a significant piece missing between these two.

I did listen to this man's videos and would highly recommend that you do as well if you run across him. But $400-700 for his course or $400 to do an hour of direct therapy with him, will most likely not provide the harmonious union he promises. He doesn't cover boundaries, codependency, or even how to communicate with an unhealed or barely healing divine counterpart.

What you should do then? Go within. Gain insight from your higher self, your spirit guides, the universe itself, and eventually even your counterpart's higher self. This is where you begin receiving information and guidance that no one else can provide you with. As you may have gathered from the first of my examples that went wrong, the coach I was working with had no experience with the amount of darkness and trauma my counterpart still has inside him. I also learned later that the divine feminine should focus on their healing specifically and not their twin's healing. Sending them love is okay, and observing their behaviors from the present or past is helpful because they are a mirror and will give you hints on what to heal. But there is no reason to channel their healing work as I did. That could have been very damaging to my psyche had I continued.

Coaches should be more for support and to help you bring out YOUR inner guidance map. For example, if you were coaching with me and asked me a question, I would ask you what you feel your options are on what to do next. Once you gave those to me, I would help you explore how each one could affect you. For example, is one decision a pattern you've already repeated, such as getting back together with your unhealed twin? What might happen if you held firm and didn't get back together with them? List 3 ways you might benefit from that. List 3 ways your twin might benefit from that. Even with that, I would want you to explore why you may resist these things and tell me what feels right to you. Even if you decided to get back together with your twin, knowing in your heart it was wrong; the universe may have wanted it to happen to show you something else you couldn't see before. There is often another lesson here. Don't feel shame about these occurrences. Don't even call them mistakes. The last time I was with my twin, he pushed me away, then ghosted me, and a few weeks later I found the information on twinflames. I had heard of them before, but I completely rejected the idea that he was anything that special to me. The universe brought us back together so that the pain of him leaving me once again would finally push me to awaken to the role he plays in my life.

Is it becoming obvious yet that there are circumstances in your life and experiences that the universe wants you to have that neither I nor anyone else knows about? If I spend an entire session with you telling you that you should follow the steps I did, what good will that do? If I tell you to do plant medicine and that particular medicine isn't calling you, OR you aren't ready for it, will it help? Most likely not. There will be things in books, articles, social media etc., that will resonate you with, and then there will be ones that don't. You will agree with every mentor you find until you don't. It's okay to take what speaks to you and leave the rest—for example, there are other gurus, like Abraham Hicks, state that healing isn't necessary. But Abraham Hicks is being channeled and has never had a human experience. They don't even know what trauma is. Esther Hicks's messages are easier to understand once a certain amount of other work is done, but they can be frustrating if you are still dealing with the effects of trauma; and Esther then says trauma has nothing to do life. One day you'll find yourself listening to a guru and wanting to understand what they are saying but find it hurts to grasp it fully. That is a sign that you will get to that level one day, but you aren't there yet. It's okay to let go of that mentor and search for a new one. You do not have to kill yourself trying to hear a message you aren't ready for. Thousands of mentors are prepared with different messages, and the universe is doing its best to lead you to them. If it's wanting you to open YouTube one more time and type in twinflames again, even though you already did that last month and came up shorthanded, try again. The universe often hides information from us until it thinks we are ready. Or, as I said previously, we may have been resisting, but now we are more open and prepared to receive.

As beneficial as it is to be by yourself and fully hear your intuition, you will, along this journey, need the help of others sometimes. If I had not had my trauma therapists, retreats, plant medicine, and breathwork ceremonies, I would not have made it to where I am now. Investing in these things that strongly call you is more valuable than a weekly talk therapy session. Online workshops are suitable too, but it's not the same as getting away from your home, meeting a new group of people interested in bettering themselves, and having the powerful facilitators touch your life in the way no one else can.

I have one more example to show you how different we are. When it comes to meditation and people in the spiritual world, how often do you run across someone who swears by it, and how often do you find someone who says they have another method that works better for them? About 99 to 1, right? Exactly. I am that one. I spent years listening to people tell me that meditation was my answer. I've tried sitting in silence, guided meditations, and different kinds of sound mediations and yet experienced nothing of what other people state happens to them. I instead get the most incredible clarity from grabbing a glass of sparkling water late at night, sitting on my couch in the dark, and asking out loud the question I want the answer to. Within an hour, I have all the information I needed and can move past whatever was holding me back. I would have never found this out if I hadn't attended a trauma therapy experience where they taught me chair therapy. I used to sit on my couch doing the chair therapy with my twin, and when that got old, I eventually just spoke to myself and my guides. Trying different therapies and then exploring them alone may be the most effective tool for finding the ways that benefit you most.

All of this information is already inside of you. When we are born, a veil is put over our eyes where we can no longer see it. When you connect with something a mentor is saying, and you have an aha moment, it is you remembering who you really are. Part of that veil lifts, and it continues to lift, making you more and more conscious every time. The more you explore, the more chance you have of remembering. After a while, it becomes fun, and you'll probably be excited about attending your next retreat because it will give you the next great insight in your life.

Getting through the beginning part, where you are just starting to heal trauma, is the most painful and lonely of all the stages. I promise it does not last. After a while, you will meet more and more twinflames, most likely online, and you will feel more a part of the community that used to seem so hard to find. You will discover ones like me who are still in separation and can fully understand how it feels to be in this spot, and you will find others who are in union and share their story of how they met, separated, awakened, and reunited. You are never alone in this process.

Speaking of never being alone, the more you focus on yourself and your goals, the more the universe will try to show you how to achieve them. Things will begin happening in your life, and it will become evident that the universe planned it that way so that it could pass you another lesson. One day the universe tricked me into being alone the entire day by enticing me to drive up to northern Arizona and look at some land I had been eyeing. I didn't interact with one person all day, even though I was supposed to meet my realtor. When I got home, I quickly learned that it was trying to pass me a message about dropping my ego altogether when it came to my counterpart. I was still holding onto pride, even though I convinced myself I wasn't. That night, my counterpart's higher self visited with me like never before. He showed me how to shed my ego and reframe any negative thoughts I might be having about him into positive ones. He showed me unconditional love, in a way I hadn't seen it before. These moments with the universe and our various guides are rare and special. And once these events begin happening to you, you realize how amazing and beautiful it is to be on the twinflame journey. Many souls on this earth will spend their entire lives seeking love and fulfillment, only to fail. You are one of the lucky ones who will be provided the guidance needed to achieve this.

CHAPTER SIX

WHAT TO DO ABOUT OBSESSIVE THOUGHTS

Instead of obsessing about why divine masculines aren't doing their work, why not trust that they are?

Learn to love your twinflame without obsession. They are only meant to be an addition, not an addiction.

~ Janineishappy
TikTok

In this chapter, I will cover reframing methods and new approaches to help with obsessive thoughts. You may be ready for this chapter; you may not be. If you haven't done trauma release work (see healing chapter #4), then this chapter may do nothing but cause you to spiritually bypass. Spiritual bypassing is when you try to enter the logical or positive arena of spirituality without first facing your shadows.

I also ask that you exercise caution even if you think you don't need healing work. You simply can't go to step B without completing step A. This is typically the same advice given about the Law of Attraction, affirmations, or manifesting. When none of those things pans out the way people try to promise they will, some will blame themselves, punish themselves, and in turn, some will feel depressed and or inadequate. You aren't insufficient as a person. It's that everything I'm about to cover will seem like foreign without uncovering your truth and shadows first. I went through this myself when I had a friend tell me I should be able to feel love and compassion for my twinflame (before I knew he was my TF), even if he ends up with someone else. Now I can see the value in that, and I know it to be the truth, but then I was trying hard to see her point and heard myself saying out loud, 'Nope, nope, nope, and nope.' If you are looking at that statement the same way I did back then, consider returning to chapter 4, review the healing suggestions, do emotional/trauma release work and then come back to this. The universe has a specific plan for your healing and ascension, so you really don't want to mess with it.

If, on the other hand, you are beginning to see the point of reframing and unconditional love, continue with this chapter.

I believe every single person who is being controlled by their thoughts should read the Untethered Soul by Michael Singer. Men, being more logical, might like Power of Now by Eckhardt Tolle as well. These books are magic beyond compare, and I will not be able to do them justice, but I will explain what they will teach you.

Your mind is not you; your ego is not you. You are the soul. The mind and the ego are tools that are supposed to be working for you. Instead, you often work for them. The ego is meant to help regulate various aspects of yourself such as instincts and animalistic desires. The brain is supposed to help you solve problems, and together they are supposed to help you achieve goals. They should be turned on *when* you ask for them. Unfortunately, they have been taught they need to be working 24/7. You can see this when the brain is keeping you awake at night. Racing, for what reason? I mean, can't you work on those problems in the morning? Are these even problems you ever need to be solving? And then on top of that, there goes your twinflame, passing through your thoughts every 2 seconds, without fail. How do you fix them, how do you fix the past, how do you fix the future? Is your twinflame thinking of you? What are they doing? Maybe if you just check their Instagram, your thoughts will stop. Wait, who are they following now? Who is liking their pictures? Is that person liking their pictures as well? Maybe if you take a shower, you can stop thinking about them? Nope. Perhaps if you go for a walk? Nope. Read a book, turn on your favorite TV program, or call a friend? Nope, nope and nope. First of all, the universe doesn't want you to forget your twinflame, so some of that will always be there. But don't worry, you will get to a place where your thoughts of them become pleasant instead of constant harassment.

When you read the Untethered Soul, it will teach you that you are not your thoughts. Next time you have a thought come up, just sit and watch it. What happens? It just stops or floats on by, right? That wasn't you. Your brain learned somewhere along the way that you like it to solve problems for you, so it keeps doing it, but it's out of control because it is doing it even when you aren't wanting it to. Next step: Do not react to the thoughts as you watch them. Do not tell them to stop. Do not be defensive. You are not the thoughts; you are the observer. For example, let's say my friend hasn't texted me in 24 hours and I have a thought that she hates me. That is not me. I don't believe that for a second. I simply know she is stressed out in life and going through many health issues and doesn't have the capacity to text as I do. But the thoughts come anyway. In this example, the ego snuck in there too. It's hurt that she didn't reply to my text yesterday, but I'm not. The more you watch the thoughts, the easier it becomes to see what is and isn't you. After some time, maybe as short as a week, the thoughts come slower, less frequent, and now you have some peace.

Different from thoughts are emotions. You can't just watch these; you must release them. Maybe you do this through meditation, or you learned how to release them from a trauma release expert. If not, here is an easy way to do it. Feel it, acknowledge it and pass it through your heart chakra. As it's passing through, breathe it out, just like it is leaving your body. Once that emotion has passed, it will never revisit you. These are simply old feelings that are stuck in your body. When you are triggered or just feeling that icky feeling in the pit of your stomach or tightness in your chest, it is nothing more than an old feeling that got stuck.

EGO

See the ego's face in this picture? It does NOT like change. It hates the unknown. So, every time you try to better yourself, it will make itself known and attempt to make you miserable. Ok, so let me explain what this looks like. Let's say you want to do any one of the following things:

- o Begin working out
- o Start eating healthier
- o Try to stop drinking
- o Leave your 9-5 and start your own business

Look at the ego face again. It does not like any of this. Why? Because it likes to stay in the comfort zone. It doesn't feel comfortable there. And now, on top of it all, you are wanting to love your twinflame unconditionally? Oh, that is going to be the toughest one of them all. But they are not healing! But they are with a karmic! But they don't love me! All illusion. All part of the soul contract. All written by your soul, so it can ascend. You can fight the ascension all you want, but life will be full of misery, suffering, and pain. You will find it extremely difficult to stay in a place of fulfillment until you surrender. Guess what, though? You get to fulfill all your dreams on this path. You might still be thinking that you want a soulmate instead of your twinflame. You are going to override the universe and go the other way. Then why are you reading this book?

The Ego Spiderweb

- Focused on actual proof, doesn't have faith in others or the universe

- Can't focus on the present. Always trying to correct the past or prepare for the future. Either depressed or anxious

- Stops you from doing what is best for you

- Constantly focused on what others think. Looks to others for validation rather than going within

- Questions your abilities, causing limiting beliefs that don't really exist

- Wants to protect you and doesn't understand why you would want to risk the life you currently have. It doesn't understand that you could be fulfilled and happy with change

- Fears change and uncertainty. Wants to stay in the comfort zone
- When you make a change, it puts you in low vibration feelings to try to get you to change back
- Wants to fix everything. Perfectionism. No gratitude

These are all the things that keep your thoughts obsessively on your twinflame. Your everyday goal should be to move out of the ego into your soul and heart. Again, don't expect this to happen overnight. It's like you have to slay the ego 57 different ways.

Ego/Mind Qualities

Me   Controlling   Jealousy Anger
Pride   Coldness   Resentment
Hostility   Complaining   Power

Doing   Victim Mode   Separation
War   Intolerance Chaos Drama
Denial. Materialism Self-Importance
Past/Future Focused

Heart/Soul Qualities

*We   Love   Humble   Unity
Happiness   Being   Gratefulness
Understanding   Spirituality
Peace   Tolerance   Forgiveness
Now Focused   Altruism
Being free and letting others be free*

The last way I recommend to get to get rid of the obsessive thoughts is through breathwork, meditation, and gratitude. I'm going to share the exact recipe I use below because it is the easiest way.

Breathwork: David Palmen on YouTube. He has a 5 minute Breathing to Boost Your Energy Naturally

Heart Chakra Meditation: davidji meditation on YouTube. 20 Minute Guided Meditation for Healing EMOTIONAL PAIN & Your HEART CHAKRA

Gratitude Journal: I personally like the one on Amazon by Clever Fox. It comes in many different colors and asks you different questions every day.

Even if, like me, you haven't been able to reach enlightenment from meditation, I guarantee doing these three things as often as you can in the morning will help keep you out of ego and in your heart.

Breathwork is known to release the feelings you have around trauma. It also reduces the stress hormones in your body. The more you practice gratitude of what you already have, the more the universe feels a higher vibration from you and wants to give you more.

In the very last chapter of this book, I will discuss changing your frame of mind to union, even before union happens. All three of these are a big part of that.

CHAPTER SEVEN

WHEN NO ONE APPROVES OF YOU BEING A TWINFLAME

"Darling, you feel heavy because you are too full of the truth. Open your mouth more. Let the truth exist somewhere other than inside your body." ~ Della Hicks-Wilson

I received this quote today in a newsletter from a fellow lightworker. It's possibly the 3rd sign I've received in the past two days that I need to stop holding in my feelings. Not being able to express yourself because of how others may feel is damaging to the psyche and the body. So, here is my message.

The only people I want to share love with in this lifetime are myself, my close spiritual friends, and my twin flame. I'm done trying to act like I can love anyone who doesn't fit just because someone else thinks I should or because society wants me to. The thought of trying to form a relationship with a soulmate or have friendships with people who aren't interested in growth makes me feel dead inside and dead to the world. My purpose in life instantly crashes into 1000 tiny pieces on a hard floor.

I am in separation from my twin flame. I am currently well into my spiritual awakening and taking the steps needed to fulfill my purpose as a lightworker through as many channels as comfortable for me. I am not sure at all where my twin is in his journey. I don't believe that will be revealed to me for some time.

One night, years ago, I sat out on my patio and felt my spirit guides telling me that my twin flame was a part of me and that our mission was to learn how to love each other in this lifetime. It was expressed that this would be a powerful mission, not a perfect one. I understood that powerful meant work and perseverance. It resonated that I came to this lifetime for this exact experience and nothing else. The last time I asked for a message from his higher being, it showed me visuals of him in a ring of trash in the ocean. He feels so exhausted and has no chance right now of getting to clean water even though he wants to. This was confirmed for me during a recent reading where my spiritual advisor pulled the trash card from her deck and noted that he has toxic influences around him. She said we are a long way off from reunion but that it will happen. That he wants this, but his ego blocks him from it. At the time of this reading, I was fully ready to accept if he wasn't my twin flame, but instead, she confirmed everything I already knew. I believe the universe held that confirmation back from me for many reasons. Until it knew I was ready to hold that information in the right way.

Here are two of the common questions and statements I receive when trying to discuss my relationship with my twin flame and the answers I've been holding back:

You have attachment issues and fear emotional intimacy, and this is the only reason you are drawn to someone who isn't right for you. I have studied attachment issues and fear of intimacy for five years. I could write several articles on what that means for the average person. I am well aware that I identify with anxious attachment and also carry some fear around love. My twin flame, through our separations, brought me to discover these things about myself, and with this awareness, I have been able to do great healing work around them. Every day is an opportunity to change my actions to create greater self-love and lessen my fear of abandonment and love. Through my inner child work, I understand the need for boundaries with him and that I must protect my inner child from anything that can hurt her. My everyday work is not about chasing someone who doesn't love me; it is about forming the healthiest relationship with myself. On the note of emotional intimacy, I disagree with people's assumptions on this one. I am a person who loves deep intimate conversation. I rarely get the opportunity for this because opportunities just don't present themselves enough, mostly because I'm an introvert and love my space and because few share this quality with me.

Don't you want to find your soulmate and have a normal life with someone? You can't wait for him. I'm worried for you. Every time this question has come up in the past, my people pleaser part has kicked in and taken over. I would blurt out something like, 'Oh, of course, I won't wait. I'm willing to go with whatever the universe will bring me.' Then I would say I would prefer to be with my soulmate instead of my twin flame. They would end the conversation by telling me I needed to be open and that the universe would guide me in the right direction. After this chat, they would feel better, and I would feel like I wanted to scream inside—my throat chakra instantly out of alignment. Here I am presented with another lesson by my twin flame. Stop being a people pleaser! Saying I want to find my soulmate or manifest a soulmate goes against every feeling in my body, in what my spirit guides have told me, and against the messages the universe has sent me already. Finding a soulmate and getting married has been something pushed on me by society since I was a little girl. It forced me to believe for years that I would be nothing without that Disney fantasy to complete me. This is not my truth. I've tried to chase that ideal for almost 30 years, and for 30 years, I kept getting punched in the gut by the universe over it. If I haven't stated it in this article yet, I shall say it now. A twin flame is a lightworker who experiences all the challenges life can offer around self-love (many of them discussed throughout this article and my blog). The twin flame partner presents and mirrors those challenges so the spiritually awakening partner can work to heal them. Once the awakened partner has done enough healing, they can spread information regarding boundaries, inner child work, self-love, etc., to others who need assistance in these areas. By the time their healing is fully accomplished, their twin's healing should be well along in the process, and the universe sparks the reunion. It truly does NOT matter if the reunion with my twin flame doesn't happen until the day before I die. It does not matter if I spend my life alone. Soulmate and marriage are not MY mission. It is my mission to help others achieve that. I feel fulfilled in that and the belief that my separation from my twin flame is about to bring on his healing. Our separation is THE most crucial part because union is the driver to keep achieving the next levels of growth. There is so much hatred in this world, and every lightworker is needed. Being a twin flame is the most beautiful thing I can possibly imagine, and I'm honored at the part I play in this connection.

This was my blog entry the day I decided I no

longer cared what anyone else thought about my life. The more you try to people please, the more you have to abandon yourself. When you speak with confidence about your twinflame journey, very few people will challenge you. Recognize though that you aren't here to get everyone to agree with you, especially when it comes to your life. When other people judge, it is more about them. In addition, the twinflame journey is something greater than the judgers. Unless a person is entirely open-minded, you will never be able to convince them of what you feel.

CHAPTER EIGHT

WHY HERMIT/COCOON PHASE IS NECESSARY

As a twinflame, you most likely have or have had issues with co-dependency, low self-esteem and boundaries. The top three problems in life and love for most people, get highlighted with twinflames.

Co-dependency is a sneaky one because we like companionship, so it is a problem in and of itself, but then also feeds the low self-esteem and boundary issues.

As a child, you possibly learned that your needs weren't important, and at least one of your parents over-glorified their problems. If you refer to the section on childhood trauma in this book, you will see that parents are NEVER supposed to inflict their problems onto their children. This is called parentification. They had a bad day or are having marital problems or are depressed, it's understandable, but the child should not be brought into the problems. The adult should find a friend, professional, or partner to discuss their issues with, never their own children. When a parent dismisses your needs as a child and pulls you into their problems, it teaches you that you are not important. It also teaches us to be heavily involved in other people's problems. Because of that, we learn not to have boundaries to protect ourselves.

As I mentioned in chapter 4, you may not even

realize you are doing this because of your unconscious programming. How does this look in an adult love relationship? It means you don't know where the lines are supposed to be drawn between you and others. It means people may continue to pull you into their problems because you are used to this happening to you. In fact, you can't even tell that something wrong is happening because it is just second nature to you. But you are unhappy, your relationships keep failing, and you can't figure out why. So, let me explain how a real relationship should look. Let's say your partner has had a bad day, and they come home and feel like discussing it with you. It's okay to give them your full attention and listen; maybe you provide them with a hug. This is where it ends.

A codependent person with low self-esteem and no boundaries will feel an overwhelming need to fix this situation for their partner; they may take the energy into their body like it is their own anguish, and maybe they won't sleep that night and continue to think on this problem the next day. They may neglect their own needs because their partner is having an issue, and if the partner is the kind of person who is also codependent, they may also knowingly or unknowingly do something to take advantage of the partner trying to help. For example, they may learn it's okay to be dismissive of the other person when they start to express needs. Or they may just lash out because they didn't want to be helped in the first place and do not know how to say no nicely. In the last case, this person also has boundary issues because it is uncomfortable for them to say no in a loving calm manner. The cycle plays out in many ways and is frustrating, usually the accommodating partner might leave because their needs never get met.

With the actions I described in the first example, it never gets this far because the partner who does the listening is not codependent, not insecure, and doesn't have boundary issues. They are supportive and comforting to their partner, but they do not take in their partner's energy, nor do they try to fix it.

What does this all have to do with time alone? A whole bunch! The fastest way to grow in the twinflame journey is to spend time away from everyone as much as possible. I am talking not only about your twinflame, but friends and family too. If you work from home, that is a bonus. If not, I would try to keep your life private from co-workers as much as possible. Am I talking about isolating yourself? Yes, indeed I am. You have been trained to seek all validation from the outside. It feels incredibly painful when it stops because you have not built yourself up from the inside yet.

Your friends, family, and anyone in your life may complain and tell you how bad it is to isolate. Ignore them, and set your boundaries.

In the spiritual and healing community, isolation during a spiritual awakening is called a hermit or cocoon phase. When in a hermit phase, you will start to discover yourself. When you begin to spend time all alone, there is no one else to influence what you do or how you spend your time. Now the things that will make you feel confident about your life will come to the surface. Odds are you were so wrapped up in your twin, chasing them, doing the things they wanted to do only. It will be a shock to your ego. It is your ego that keeps you tied to something you don't like. It is used to receiving validation from others, and when things go quiet, it gets upset. When anything in your life changes, the ego feels affected. This could put you into a dark night of the soul, or it could just be that for one to three days or a week you feel not yourself.

You need to allow the ego to go through this, don't react to it, and try to not use coping mechanisms to distract from it. Just allow it to pass through the heart and be more restful during this time. Anytime you bring change into your life, you need to allow the ego to let it go of the past in its own way. Do NOT take this as a sign to return to the way you were or return to your old patterns. It's a short-term thing. This is another way reprogramming the subconscious helps.

Being alone at first feels hard. When you stop initiating things with other people, you may find they also stop initialing things with you. You may find that some of your friendships were more one-sided than you thought and that you were carrying most of the weight. At first, when you never hear your phone make the sound of a text message arriving, you will probably experience FOMO. You will be tempted to write a text to someone, anyone, just to have them respond and quickly get that void filled inside of you. If you have trouble going one weekend without texting anyone, this is an area you need to heal and you need this time alone. It doesn't matter what the activities are that you are doing, just as long as no one else participates with you. I spent over a year remodeling my house by myself. Picking out paint colors and home accents without needing the opinion of anyone else showed me #1 What I want matters #2 That my wants exist outside of anyone else's #3 That I can create great things by myself #4 That I can handle challenges by myself #5 That I didn't NEED anyone else.

This is the beginning of your transformation.

You leave codependency behind and you feel free. The world is now yours. When you are codependent on a partner for everything, you won't take a vacation alone, and therefore, you may miss out on the dream vacation of your lifetime. Is that how life is supposed to be? Hell no. Time alone shows you that YOU matter and eventually you won't care if people are around or not. This is vital to your life because, at the end of the day, you are the only person you can count on. It sounds harsh to hear that at first, but it really is the truth and once you have been alone for a while, it doesn't seem harsh, nor does it hurt or feel painful in any way. In fact, things feel better because you can fulfill your own needs and desires anytime you want to. You are waiting on no one and the world now shows you everything that is open to you.

Being alone starts the connection with your spirit team. When you are around people all the time, all you hear is them. Even when you are in the car alone, you probably hear on repeat in your mind what they have said to you about what they think. You never get space to hear from your higher self or the universe. Or the universe may be trying to get you alone to provide you with a download, but you don't take the opportunity because going out with a friend for a drink sounds better than being alone. See what you miss out on?

You miss out on yourself. Remembering who you are. You probably started to express what you wanted when you were little. Either you were told no by your parents because they saw money as limited, or they just didn't care about your desires. Or you couldn't do that thing because school took up too much time. The schools we are forced to attend are created around making us good little worker bees that will sit behind a desk and do what we are told by management who can never seem to see our side of things, no matter how nice they seem. What if you were never made to learn algebra, calculus, chemistry, accounting, or physics? You'd still be here, right? Doing exactly what you are doing today? I mean unless you are an engineer or a bio-nuclear physicist. Reading, writing, and basic math were all we really needed from school. The rest should have been up to us to decide on.

When you are an adult and you begin your alone time, you get to start all that over again. Have you thought about your dreams yet? Do you want to pick out some fabulous paints and a canvas and paint the day away in front of a window? Do you want to do some adrenaline-seeking adventure? Do you want to sit at the pool? Start swimming laps? Ride a horse? Write a song? Do a full day of self-care? Veg and watch movies all day? Practice new things like gratitude, breathwork or meditation? Go on a day trip somewhere? Rent an exotic car or motorcycle, scooter, ATV? Do you see it yet? The world is your oyster and you were chosen as one of the souls to come to earth and experience this messy, beautiful damn thing we know as life. Doesn't twinflame separation seem minor in comparison? That's because it is. This is where your happiness lies and this is how you reprogram how you live your entire life. When you remove all the limiting blocks, it's now all yours.

When this finally happened for me, I went to an Ayahuasca retreat in Costa Rica by myself, quit my 9-5, wrote this book, became a content creator, an artist, started my own huge garden, and built my days entirely around me. It's hard to see when you are stuck back in a place where all that matters is your twinflame. So, you need to climb yourself out of there. That place won't get you back into union with them. Why? Because you aren't in union with yourself yet.

Your twin, believe it or not, knows that you are part of the divine, but they will leave you alone until YOU see it and until you live it. This is why they say exes always come back when you moved on. But here's a little secret: you aren't moving on from them, they just don't know that. Instead, you are moving more INTO yourself and holding unconditional love for them. That's where the magic is. It's in you already. You are the only one who can bring it to the surface. Your higher self knows this, so do your spirit guides, the universe, and your twin's higher self as well. They are all trying to extend that offer to you to open the door to yourself and to your life.

Here is my recollection of my spiritual awakening and being alone:

I don't even know how long I've been in my spiritual awakening. I'm not even sure how to define when it began. Was it the day I woke up and decided to leave my ex-fiancé because I decided there had to be more to life? Was it the day that I decided to book my first retreat? Or maybe the day when I decided I had father issues that needed to be unearthed, so I could stop ruining my dating life?

I know that the further I go into my spiritual awakening, the more private my life has and has had to become. When you spend less time in the matrix and come into consciousness, many things will begin to change. The changes that occurred this year almost had me thinking I would become 'boring.' No drama, no alcohol, no late nights, no toxic men. But the me that came from that feels peaceful and confident, and I can see rainbows all around me.

Most of the struggle is losing most of the people

in your life and the others who remain; you lose your closeness with them. Why? Your spiritual awakening cannot come to fruition without this step of climbing the mountain. You simply won't reach the peak of where you are meant to be if you try to keep all these people with you. You are only as good as the average of the people around you, so keeping them means keeping yourself stuck where they are at.

I tried it both ways. I tried to keep them close to me, and then I tried my life more in isolation, and I found I couldn't hear my soul with them so close. I understand everyone is doing their absolute best in life and that they constantly want to share their best and how you should be following their lead, but their thoughts, it turns out, are nothing but noise in my mind. Let's face it, everyone has an opinion regarding everything, and that's great. But during my spiritual awakening, I just wish I had friends who knew how to listen, so I could share without them clouding my thoughts. This, unfortunately, isn't possible as I've lost friendships when trying to share these simple needs. These days, I keep those thoughts to myself, spend an awful lot of time alone, and check in from time to time on those that I care about.

This isn't sad to me. My mind is filled with everything I can now manifest in my life. My twinflame, the career I want, rejuvenate some of my old hobbies I got away from in the past and find some new ones. Travel to places I've wanted to go to for years. And finally, manifest my soul tribe. The friends who have found or are finding their purpose, the ones who aren't in the matrix 24/7, the ones who aren't scared to up-level or go on new adventures and travel with me. The ones who aren't scared to be alone. The ones who believe they can do and be anything they want in life. Because that's who I am now, and I'm ready for the people that can match my newfound energy.

I will look back and know all of this was worth it one day. Every moment alone to find me and exactly who I am is what allowed my dreams to flourish. It will allow me to look back on my life and see that I had everything I ever wanted.

When you have mastered being alone, you master not caring what anyone else thinks.

CHAPTER NINE

WHY YOUR COUNTERPART
NEEDS YOU TO HEAL

I see it every single day. There is always a divine feminine saying, 'Why do I have to do healing work when they aren't making an effort. I'm done, out, and moving on to someone who doesn't have these issues.' Most of us have been here at one time or another. It seems unfair from where we sit, seeing them date karmics, still cater to karmic members of their family, or dedicate themselves to addictions. Healing isn't easy. Facing our shadows and our ego is the most challenging work we will ever do. And on top of that, it has to be done alone. I remember seeing my twin post a picture of himself with a picture cred and a heart for the woman he was dating. He wrote about how happy he finally was in life. I was beyond angry. I felt like I had been to hell and back doing healing work. I faced addictions I never thought I could. I put all my money and time into bettering myself. When I wasn't at a retreat, I was doing an online course, listening to podcasts, and reading books to improve myself. It consumed my life. I hadn't even seriously dated anyone else. And here he was, my twin, who had done no work on himself, hadn't faced one single shadow, dealt with his addictions, apologized to me, or forgiven me. I was hurt, enraged, and cursed at the universe for its unfairness. I pointed this out to a longtime friend, and she simply stated, 'Nothing on Instagram is as it appears.' Two weeks later, they broke up. And two weeks after that, he left a note on my door wanting to speak with me.

I tell you this story to point out that my friend was right; things are never as they appear. If your twin is acting like things are great, they aren't. If they give the Oscar award-winning performance of their life that they don't need to heal and are happy, it is just that, a performance. You can only cover up pain and trauma with addictions and a new partner for so long. The same 2x4s that have come along to hit you in the head will do the same with your counterpart. It is only a matter of time. And, it's not for you to point out to them either. They will see it on their own. If you try to point it out, their ego will fight back harder. But if you just let the universe take care of it with its 2x4s and maybe every now, and then a MAC semi-truck hitting them full force, the job will get done better than you could have done it anyway. Bonus, you don't have to look like the bad guy. You let the universe take that role. The thing you need to remember here is that the 3D is an illusion. It's an experience. It's a storyline you chose before you were incarnated to earth. As one soul, with your counterpart, you BOTH chose this. It's just that you have woken to this and they haven't yet. You were handed part of the script. You can't see all of it. Our guides and the universe don't like to give us everything at once. It takes the fun and thrills out of it. I mean, you don't go to see a movie knowing how it will end, do you? You would just stay home. If you are a twinflame, you are here because you are an old soul, and this is one of the last, if not the last, lifetime you will encounter. The twinflame journey is the most challenging and hardest one to pass. If you and your twin pass it in this lifetime, you don't return to do it again.

You are not going to forget about your counterpart, and the universe is not going to let you just swing by without any more of the 2x4s or synchronicities. You will feel pain, suffering, loneliness, and misery until you surrender to the journey, your twin, and the work. It is your choice. I write this book for all of you because I surrendered and no longer suffer. My entire purpose in this lifetime is to talk with all of you about why it is better to realize this is the challenge you chose; this is the exact storyline you picked. You and your counterpart, as one soul, experienced a split and then forgot who you are or what this was all about. You will find out otherwise after being beaten up by the lessons enough.

Often, when a divine feminine comment on one of my TikTok's about how unfair this is, I remind them that someone has to go first. I played the tit-for-tat game with my twin for five years, which got us nowhere. One day, I had a download hit me that the only way this would work was if I healed first, if I said no to participating in any more drama, and if I genuinely became the picture of someone who has entered their divine stage.

If both of you stay in the immature, fearful stage of this journey, you will continue to be forced into separation. No one will ever be vulnerable, forgive or be emotionally available. It will just stay the same as it's always been. You know that isn't what you want. In fact, I am willing to bet you've already told the universe what you want, right?

At some point along the way, you wished for one or more of the following:

- A loyal, trusting relationship
- To feel secure and confident within yourself
- To enjoy your counterpart but not need them
- To know what real love is
- To understand what self-love feels like
- To have your counterpart want to be a part of your life without you demanding it or having to ask for it constantly
- For your counterpart and you to be in space where you are both growing
- To know your counterpart loves you, even when they are not present or tangibly showing they love you
- To have a relationship that is not codependent

- To be free of the anxious attachment feelings that make you check on your counterpart constantly

Sound familiar? Even if you haven't realized it yet, you've been manifesting this. Maybe you said it out loud; perhaps it was just what entered your thoughts when you were frustrated facing another separation. Either way, it's your desire, and believe it or not, your counterpart's desire. However, your counterpart is still in the phase where they feel it is too difficult to get there, near impossible. They either feel like they just can't do it, or they've exhausted themselves trying. They've never had a good example of a relationship and aren't called to find those examples like you are. Not yet, anyway. Do you know who will become their example one day?

Yes…you. I know it will take time. You will need to step fully into the divine feminine that is ready to receive. That is why your separation has been as long as it has. You have to be so strong that you can't be triggered by them anymore, or if the trigger occurs, you know how to go to your safe, quiet space and regain your strength. You have to be able to look at the situation for what it is.

In chapter 1, we looked at the differences between the divine and the wounded masculine/feminine.

A step further can be taken by looking at the 3rd, 4th and 5th dimensions. This involves the feelings that you may have alone or in a relationship.

The 3rd dimension includes feelings such as:

Sad   Afraid/Fear   Jealous
Hurt   Doubt   Dishonesty
Vengeful   Unforgiving   Negative
Judgmental   Unworthy   Controlling
Defensive

As you move into the 4th dimension, you will feel more of these feelings:

Secure   Enthused   Confidence
Grateful   Empowered   Focused
Positive   Courageous   Tolerant
Relieved   Giving   Worthy
Happy   Understanding   Forgiving

When you live in these 4th dimension feelings, you let go of suffering. You let go of separation feeling like it's bad or a punishment. It is an accomplishment alone to get to 4th dimension feelings. Once you start to ascend and form a greater relationship with the divine, you will tap into the 5th dimension feelings.

5th dimension feelings:

Infinite   All-knowing   At peace
Unconditional love   Awakened
Oneness   Aware   Accepting

Here are some examples of what this looks like. Let's say someone criticizes you, and you acknowledge the criticism and defend yourself or try to prove to the person that they are wrong. You have now rewarded them and encouraged them to do it again. When you see your twin enter any of the 3D actions, you cannot enter there with them. My favorite trauma therapist once told me, 'He will get on the roller coaster, just don't get on it with him.' If you join on the roller coaster, neither of you will be able to break free of it. It seems that's all they know, and they are scared to try any other way because you are fearful of the unknown.

Let's turn the tables with the person that provided the criticism. Let's say you don't acknowledge it. Don't be a people pleaser, and don't try to cover it up for them either. You just let the silence fall to them. Can you see how their ego didn't receive the reward it wanted? Can you see how it turns back on them, and now they feel like a jackass because you aren't giving them any choice but to sit in the silence, and an instant reflection will come up, whether they like it or not. The reflection will say something like, 'Way to go, you just brought up unloving negativity' or 'Wow, way to go, sir, you didn't just earn any points with that comment.' It's the same when your counterpart gets on the roller coaster, and you don't join them. Then they are alone with their own drama.

Here is an example of mine that failed miserably. I reached out to my twin because I had been listening to a new workshop that convinced me that if I could just remain in a state of happiness and fulfillment at all times, no one else could affect me or even trigger me. This was before I knew about twinflames, so I didn't have the whole story, but I convinced myself I did. I also didn't know about twinflame triggering or how triggers are a sign of me needing to heal. So, we spoke for a few weeks. I tell him all I need to know is that he's not involved with anyone else. He says he's not, and everything seems like it might work out this time.

There was a lot more at play here than I realized, but the part I'm focusing on is what came next. He didn't text me for ten days. I didn't get mad. I didn't even say anything about it. I entirely acted like it hadn't been TEN FULL DAYS. One day I went on Instagram, and he posted a picture of himself in a freestanding tub of a hotel room. Although you couldn't see all of him, you knew he was in the tub naked. There was a bed in the background with sheets all messed up on it, and from how the picture was taken, you could tell it must have been taken by whomever he had been in that bed with. I don't even need to explain how that trigger felt. I immediately texted him and said something to the effect of 'I thought you said you weren't sleeping with anyone else.' He knew exactly what I was talking about and, to further make my blood boil, took about 30 minutes to answer me before saying, 'That picture was taken a year ago.' The next day we were back in separation.

Okay, step back here for a minute and just observe how we do this. How our twin can post a stupid picture, and our buttons get pressed so hard we can't unstick them. If you sit back and look at that particular situation with an understanding of trauma, you can understand so much more. My twin does not normally post pictures like that. He hadn't posted them when they were taken and hasn't posted anything remotely like that in the year since it happened. Why then? Why pull that picture out of the history files right then and post it for the public to see? On top of that, posting a caption that read 'Can't keep a toxic white male down.'

In the time that I've had to reflect on this without the triggering, I see this differently. When I had first contacted him, he kept saying, 'I can't give you what you need.' I brushed it off because I thought I wouldn't let that bother me anymore, so I didn't listen to him and still wanted to see him. By posting this picture, it was his way of subconsciously posting an even bigger flag with bright shining lights saying, 'I'm not good enough for you, I can't give you what you need.' He just did it in a way where I could no longer ignore it. To add to that, his higher self was 100% watching this play out and even supporting it. The fact that I kept pushing to stay with him highlighted my lack of self-love and self-disrespect. Do you see how your twin is always mirroring you? Your twin is not conscious as to why they are doing this, but their higher self sees and knows it all. They are trying to protect you. Both know you deserve better.

Before your twin is healed, they have a skewed, incorrect perception of themselves. They see how others have treated them, and that is what they believe they are. My twin fully sees himself as a toxic white male and nothing else. Even though the soul knows your twin is different, they are not yet in touch with that yet. Everything is still being controlled by the subconscious mind that repeats, 'You aren't good enough.'

On top of that, the subconscious also tells them everyone is out to hurt them, and they can trust no one. They may have no inkling of what love is. In the next chapter, I will cover more about when to accept this person back into your life and when not to. Over time in your healing, though, you will also be able to decide for yourself the best way to accept them back.

If I had known everything back then that I know now, I would not have reacted to that trigger. I would have seen it for what it was. An insecurity he acted on by pushing me away. He jumped on the roller coaster, and I jumped on with him. I didn't need to, and I shouldn't have.

Your twin is showing you your own lack of self-love and unworthiness; your twin is showing you your imprisonment to the mind and the ego. They didn't stick around to continue to take advantage of you. They left or ghosted because they know you are self-love, you are infinite, you are divine and you are free. But it's you who doesn't see that. You're not going to hear from your twin again until you've done this. And if they come back before they themselves have healed, it is only because the universe feels you need another 2x4 lesson. It's testing you again. Do you see how worthy you are? A high priestess? Are you willing to set the boundaries in the way a high priestess would?

Only through proper example and serious boundaries is your twin going to see that they are, in essence, being ridiculous. That they are a slave to old patterns. When you don't join them on the roller coaster and are seriously consistent in the person you have become, you no longer enable their bad behavior, ego, or disrespect of you. But I said it before, and I repeat it: You have to go first. Get off the roller coaster and don't even enter the theme park. Your twin wants out of the theme park too. I'm sure at some point you've heard them say they don't want the drama anymore. It's because they don't, but change is difficult. Anyone caught up in an unhealthy masculine identity has been taught by society that they are doing nothing wrong and the ego backs it.

'Don't show emotion' and 'Grow some balls' has led us to a society full of emotionally unavailable people. Even as a little girl, my dad used to punch me on the arm in a playing manner, and I would ask him why he did that. He always told me, 'I'm making you strong.' But he never told me he loved me or communicated vulnerable feelings with me. This is what your counterpart has been conditioned to be. And when you try to tell them otherwise, you are outside banging on a window that is 100 panes thick, and they can't hear you. You must allow the universe to show them through various karmic lessons that this is not who they are. That they are love, just like you have learned that you are. When they begin to awaken, they need to see that you have moved past the trauma and no longer subscribe to unworthiness. That you no longer partake in drama or addictions. Although the universe will be doing most of the work, they will see a little tiny light shining in you, and the more consistent you are with it, the brighter the light gets until one day they can no longer deny the healed version of you.

If you are still thinking, 'Ya, but what if they don't?', you have some more work regarding your relationship with uncertainty. Your ego wants things to be certain and wants to convince you as much as possible that you need to see proof that your counterpart will heal before you buy-in. You need to remember that your ego was matrix influenced. It has been conditioned to disregard faith, and it also works hard to keep you a slave to it. You need to flip the switch and remind the ego that it works for you, just like the mind. Your inner child, ego, and mind don't lead your life. You lead your life.

When you form a bond with uncertainty and surrender to the universe, doors begin to open in your life that you could never have imagined. The reason you couldn't imagine it before is that you were raised with limiting beliefs. Society told kept you down low where you couldn't open doors. You don't have to stay there. The universe doesn't want you there. Other people in your life will stay there, and you will need to leave them there. But you are a twinflame, and the universe has a much greater mission for you. For you and your counterpart. You were given the role of being awakened, of knowing. It's no coincidence that you are now reading this book and being asked to leave your old self behind. The universe provided these downloads to me to be written and provided to you at the exact moment you are reading it. 'When the student is ready, the teacher appears.' It is just that simple.

This is why I call us 'Twinflame Royalty.' The twinflame journey is arduous - the most challenging journey you will face. You deserve to wake up in the morning and feel good about your role in this lifetime and that the universe is conspiring to bring you and your twin back together if you are willing to surrender to the faith of it all.

Last words of caution that all twinflames must know about their counterparts:

- Your only responsibility is to heal yourself and set an example of the light
- The minute your counterpart lowers your vibration; it is a sign that you need a new boundary in place
- You, yourself, cannot heal them; they must decide to do the work
- Your counterpart can only love you as deeply as they love themselves
- When you surrender to the twinflame journey, you must also surrender the desire to 'fix' your twin. Meaning you tell your ego that it does not even begin to know what lessons or healing gurus your twin needs. You relinquish all to the higher power, and your twin's higher self to show them the way.
- You hold firm with your inner knowing that you are Queen or King, and no one, not even your twin can take that from you.

CHAPTER TEN

WHAT YOU NEED TO KNOW ABOUT THE DIVINE MASCULINE (RUNNER)

LETTER TO MY UNAWAKENED TWINFLAME

I'm trying to figure out why I want to write to you. I only used to write out of pain or ego, and I don't have much of that left, so here goes an entirely different kind of letter.

You will begin to go through something you never have before in the next few years. You may have always felt drawn to spirituality and escaping the matrix, but it will feel incredibly powerful when the divine comes calling. You will be pulled towards it in ways you couldn't even imagine. Something will probably happen with your job. Either you'll burn out, you won't want to be there, or you'll sabotage it somehow. This will make no sense since it is the job you always wanted. Regardless, you'll no longer fully fit there.

Any friends you may have will no longer give you any reason to want to be around them. You'll feel empty with them like something is missing. You might try to have deep conversations about this new thing you are experiencing, and they just won't be able to go there with you, even if they try to act like they are.

You'll start to feel pain wanting to be addressed. The porn, the overworking, and the pot won't push down the pain successfully anymore. They won't be satisfying coping mechanisms like they used to be. For a while, you might still have an on-again, off-again relationship with them, but they won't feel as good as they did before. You will realize you want to let go of these things.

Because of this, you may feel like you just want to be alone more. It is your soul asking you to stop focusing on the external quite so much and go within. You might feel like you are starting to figure out new things about yourself, like aha moments. It will feel like a light, like magic that you've never felt before. This is you remembering who you are. For the first time, your intuition might get louder. You won't know it yet, but there will be guidance coming from the universe, your spirit guides, your higher self, and even my higher self.

I see your higher self as half Jason Bateman, half genie. A lot of the time, he is laughing. He laughs at the human experience we are having. He laughs at us in separation and how we take everything so seriously, how we try to be perfect, or push each other away. He laughs because he knows we are one soul, and we can't get any closer than that, but we still think we are so far from each other because the 3D illusion makes us believe we are.

My higher self's name is Alyssa. There is always

wind blowing through her perfect hair. She is always having fun; she is carefree. She craves adventure but is always happy and will create adventure anytime. She doesn't laugh like your higher self, but she is always smiling, she knows that everything is good, and everything always will be good. She knows things are brighter than we can see. She is a goddess of light who worries about nothing.

They both know we have to go through specific experiences before meeting again. We planned certain karmic lessons as one soul before we reincarnated. As I go through this, I see myself choosing those karmic lessons less and less. You will, too, once you realize what is happening.

This is your spiritual awakening. It is you coming back to our soul. Believe it or not, we are all waiting here for you. Me, your future soul tribe of twinflames, your guides, the universe. We all know it's just a matter of time before you come back to yourself and me. Whatever you are going through now, even if you are seeing someone else – it's just part of the process. There are lessons there that will eventually bring you into alignment.

It will take time, but eventually, you will start to let go of many things. You'll stop caring what people think of you. You'll start doing whatever the fuck you want. You'll be okay with ending the friendships you no longer need. You'll probably begin to see your aunt for what she really is and how she manipulates you. Your relationship with her signifies some feminine wounding you need to heal. Some things may take longer to let go of than others.

When you see me again, you'll see a difference. You may try to imagine the old me still surviving, but you'll soon see that the low vibrational energy that used to exist between us will no longer be tolerable. Or should you choose to engage in it, you won't see me join you. You'll start to see more of Alyssa in me. And you might even be able to pick up on the unconditional love I feel for you.

This is all going to seem crazy at first. Not all of what I just spoke of will come to fruition right away, and the changes that do come will be piece by piece. It won't make sense, and because you no longer fit in anywhere, you might think something is wrong with you. But there is nothing wrong with you. You are going through the exact experience you should be.

And then there is the twinflame connection. This will seem to be the strangest of all. I mean, you let go of me. You told me to stop texting you. So why are you still thinking about me all this time later? No matter what other woman you are with, you can't just move past us. Maybe you'll start to see that you have been trying to replace me and have failed.

Perhaps you will notice that the house you have created for yourself mirrors a lot about my home. In small weird ways, they are very similar. And the ways they aren't alike kind of bothers you. This is all because you never really left me, and I never really left you. You felt it in your soul and couldn't help but try to have whatever of me that you possibly could. You knew you couldn't be with me because I wanted to make you face things you weren't ready to. And it doesn't matter because the universe has told me it is walking with you. It will help you bring to the surface the same things I was trying to, but now you will be ready.

It has to come from within you and your relationship with spirit. I support you. Sometimes, I lay beside you and allow my love to be an amber glow that hugs you. Other times, I think of what I went through during my spiritual awakening and how it all ended up for the best. Then I try to send you that hopeful energy to lessen the pain if at all possible.

It was strange at first, knowing all this will happen to you at some point, but I also felt incredibly happy knowing you would heal. Long before I knew what twin flames were, spirit told me that, well, actually, it's something that is too hard to put into words. Let's just say spirit showed us healing together. With the twin flame journey, we are supposed to do most of this work apart, but we will still have some healing experiences together. I just don't know what they are yet and will leave it to the universe to decide what that will be. It knows what we need, and it knows when we need it.

You are protected, you are loved, and you will learn to exist without suffering or pain. It's all coming. I love you.

MASCULINE HEALING

The men that exist today mostly fall into two categories. One where they identify too much with the wounded masculine and reject the feminine inside them. They are the typical avoidant or emotionally unavailable guys. The other is the nice guy. This guy is taught to deny his masculinity and overcompensates for the feminine around him. He is not really nice because he does nice things only to get something in return. You generally may be friends with this guy, but you will never respect him.

To further illustrate the issues the divine masculine faces today, here is how Sarah Elkhaldy, aka, The Alchemist on YouTube, defined them:

- The matrix wants to mold him into the

image of the false masculine

- Shamed out of his feelings; knocked out of his emotional body
- His sex drive is targeted to keep him out of his higher centers
- With nowhere for his energy to go, it is blocked in his root center, creating a limited identity of his full potential
- He is suppressed by forces that look like they are for him. They don't want him to step into his inner authority. Brainwashed to believe he is an instrument for pathological forces only
- His sex drive has been overexploited through the porn they have pumped into his psyche.

In other words, he is completely disconnected from who he is and is working off of his unhealed masculine/feminine energies to the tune of what the matrix wants from him.

If you want to get an extreme idea of what the divine masculine goes through when running, read The Truth by Neil Strauss. If you are going to read the book and don't want the ending spoiled, skip to page 203 now. This is not a twinflame story, but it is a true story showcasing exactly what the masculine goes through, including karmic lessons.

When he first became famous, Neil wrote The Game, a book about how to pick up women. He was self-taught. One day he didn't know how to talk to a woman, and the next, he was teaching others how to do just that. He eventually fell for a woman named Ingrid, but his pickup days were not behind him, and he cheated on her. Hoping not to lose her, he put himself into sex rehab for a while, but when he got out, he was back at it, texting other women in no time. He was convinced that being in a relationship with Ingrid was a prison. He was the perfect example of the type of man that would be classified as a 'cheating narcissist.'

Ingrid was livid and he ran from her, not looking back. He was now on a mission to try polyamory. He found himself with three girlfriends. They were practically waiting for him in his Rolodex of women. Keep in mind here; the divine masculine becomes super convinced that you were just the wrong choice, and they think they know better.

But his live in foursome turned into a disaster. This is the beginning of his karmic lessons, #1.

He now had three women demanding his time instead of one. One of the women couldn't control her jealousy and spent more time crying and being sad than happy with him.

During this time, he explored it all, including sex clubs in LA and polyamory retreats. He then decided to break it off with all three women and sought a relationship with one woman who would be willing to be with him as a couple but still allow them both 'time' with other people as needed. It went well for a while until it came time for her to sleep with other men. He watched her flirt with someone else in a bar one night and found he didn't exactly like how he felt in this scenario. He asked for an open relationship, but he had obviously not thought this whole thing through. Then she decided to take a trip to Mexico with two other men. While she was gone, Neil would wait hours or days just to get a text from her. He got to see exactly what he had done to Ingrid, although in this case, there wasn't much he could do about it because he had fully agreed to this relationship, even the part where his partner would be fucking other men. This was his karmic lesson #2.

Interestingly, in this book, Neil had a friend named Rick, who was full of knowledge about relationships and working on oneself. Rick is a reasonably central character in this book, giving Neil advice constantly about how he should reconsider his actions. That he shouldn't have left Ingrid and that whomever he is with, he should take things slower and not make it all about sex. It is fascinating to hear Rick's profound knowledge, and yet Neil is still so determined to do what he wants, what he is convinced will make him happy in life.

He literally can't hear Rick; he is still asleep. That is until not being able to reach his girlfriend in Mexico. It made him sit alone with his feelings and what he had done. He thought about calling up one of his other hookup partners to fill the void, but he knew deep down that wouldn't make him feel fulfilled or satisfied. He was downright hurt. On top of that, he realized that he would never be able to have children with this woman. Kids were important to him, and he did not want to be put into a situation where he had to explain why their mother was away in Mexico with other men. It was at this very moment that Neil woke up.

By the time she was back from Mexico, he was ready to express his needs to her about total exclusivity and wanting to have children. She did not return those desires. Instead, she wanted to keep doing exactly what she was doing. Their relationship ended, and guess whom Neil decided he wanted back? Yep, Ingrid. She was everything he wanted but before, he couldn't see it.

As you go through the rest of this story with him in the book, you follow him on a Machu Picchu backpacking trip with just one of his buddies from sex rehab and a mountain guide. He decides on this trip that upon returning to the US, he would go back to the same place where he had gone through sex rehab, but this time enter programs around love addiction and childhood trauma. He discovered the reasons he couldn't commit to Ingrid stemmed from being enmeshed with his mother.

He was determined to try to get Ingrid back, but even more determined he would not show up back in her world until he had done the work on himself. He even carefully planned out three unique gifts to give her. She had no idea any of this was going on until the day he finally approached her. I will leave the rest for you to read in the book. It is a very entertaining book and the same book that led me to do healing work at the same place he did.

You will see why it takes the divine masculine so long in separation. Think about your resistance in letting go of the ego, trusting the universe, and letting go of the drama and bad friends in your own life. I believe the ego is even stronger in the masculine, and if you try to make them see something before they are ready, the ego will fight you even harder. You kind of become the enemy to the DM's ego.

Now, it's not all ego that is pushing you away. There is some insecurity and low self-worth. Neil was a prime example. He became a pickup artist to hide his low self-worth, but it was still there, underneath the surface. He just stuffed it down. And this is what a lot of DMs are doing—not facing their shit until it gets thrown in their faces.

I wrote this chapter so that you understand what must happen on their side. The demons they must slay. You simply can't be a part of that. You have to surrender to the universe and let it happen.

I have another story for you—my own. I was the divine masculine once. When I met my twin, I had not done any healing work, did not know I was a twinflame, still had my addictions controlling me, and was not ready to be a good partner. I was very involved in my career and had a very close best friend, a guy who unconsciously stood in the way of me ever having a successful relationship. See the perfect recipe for disaster? Being a mirror of me, my twin came into the relationship with very low self-esteem. He didn't have many friends, didn't have his career started, and latched on to me. Although I seemed to be greatly independent, on the inside, I was a very insecure person who was covering up all that was wrong with me. My twin became very jealous of the other guys who liked talking to me in the car club we were both a part of. Even though I wasn't interested in any of those other guys, nor were they interested in me (to my knowledge anyway), he still acted out with false accusations and jealousy. He couldn't stand how busy I was with my career and my best friend. I was determined to not change those things because I wanted to take things slow with him, and I thought that was helping – to keep my life as it was. My twin expressed more and more how angry/upset this made him to not have more time with me. I asked if he wanted to move in. I had convinced myself that maybe he would be happier that way. But because he didn't have a life outside of me, it just meant that he was still unhappy, but now unhappy in my house. A week later, I asked him to leave. He was so incredibly hurt. I don't believe I've ever seen someone in that much pain in my life, other than myself. I had started studying CPTSD before meeting him, and knew this was his childhood trauma, but since I hadn't even healed my trauma yet, I had no idea how to support him. I mean, I could have just sat him down on the couch and hugged him and let him cry. I was not emotionally available to do so. I thought I remembered still wanting to see him on the weekends but needing a break. He seems to remember that I ghosted him. This is what happens between twinflames. Triggering to the nines, and neither one even recalls the same story. But in the end, I ran. My life coach told me I should date other people, so I did. Did I think about my twin? He wasn't completely gone from my mind, but I didn't know how to make it work, and no one around me wanted me with him. Back in those days, I needed validation from others. I couldn't think for myself yet. On top of that, I hadn't yet mastered the art of being alone, so I ran back to a man I used to date who had cheated on me before. I, like Neil, decided I would try polyamory, and then this guy could do what he wanted and still be honest with me. Like Neil, I was convinced I could find a solution without my twin. This pilot ex of mine was my karmic lesson. And to make it worse, he later broke my twin and me completely apart. This happened after I fell deeply in love with my twin and wanted nothing but a life with him. All runners think they are doing the right thing at the time. They have no idea what is waiting for them as they proceed in this direction.

The main thing to take from these two stories is that the bad, hurtful stuff must play out. Your divine masculine will learn, like Neil and I did, through their mistakes.

You can always ask spirit for advice. You can also channel where your divine masculine is at in the journey. You won't get details like social media is

WHAT YOU NEED TO KNOW ABOUT THE DIVINE MASCULINE

going to give you. You'll get the truth. And it's not always what you think. You probably think your counterpart hates you or doesn't think of you. If you stay in the ego and the mind too long, that is what you will become to believe. Around the time of the publishing of this book, I asked my team to do some channeling for me and the divine feminine. The answers I received were not at all what I was expecting. The messages said that at the time of the soul contract, the part of our soul that was to be the divine masculine would protect the divine feminine during their healing. The dark night of the soul for the masculine will be far worse than for the feminine and they won't take that step until they know the divine feminine is okay. Until then, they are numb, they stay in their addictions, be it work, a karmic partner, porn, alcohol, weed, you name it. As long as they are numb, they can hold an energetic bubble of protection around you. They sacrifice for you and they aren't pushing you either. They will do this as long as necessary, but your spirit team feels differently. They will push you. And you can't bullshit them either. You can't just say 'I'm ok, the divine masculine can proceed with healing now.' You have to do the work and you have to be authentic about this. Then and only then will the divine masculine feel that you will stay on safe ground while they face their demons. Your spirit team will be subtle most times, but the voice is clear if you are open to receiving it. I still swear by healing, trauma release from the body, and plant medicine, but nothing takes your team's place. We can't just be with a trauma release expert every day or be at an Ayahuasca ceremony every day. Your spirit team is with you every single day, without fail. Sometimes you will forget about them, and it will affect your day, and then you will know it's time to sit with them.

I just want to add one small section on men attempting to work towards their divine masculine. I know this part won't apply to all divine feminines reading this book, but I feel it will apply to most and is worth reviewing. A few things, not twinflame journey or karmic lesson related affect the men we love so very much.

#1 Most divine masculines are delayed because they are waiting for success in their career, buying a house, or maybe finding their purpose. Men know and feel the need to provide for their divine feminine in their bones. It may not seem obvious just yet, especially if they are still asking you to pay the dinner check 50/50, but it's there. It's just like us women, having a common issue of being primarily in our masculine but still wanting to feel safe and protected by him. We have to get in our feminine to get that from a man, and he needs to get into his masculine to want to provide it fully. Again, he may not see it, but he has the urge; he is being driven to achieve these things before committing to the divine feminine.

#2 The divine masculine has no time to feel love - he just feels fear and runs – they feel all these unusual feelings that they cannot pin down. Guilt, sadness, shame, and feelings of unworthiness then project all these demons on the twin. It's the twin that made them run - run out of fear (of love). This is what they think, but they are running from themselves.

Are you starting to see yet why you don't have a role to play in any of this? Why divine feminines who have found happiness on this journey tell you to focus on you, your healing, and your purpose? Not only is that what is best for you, but there is nothing else you can do. At the beginning of your separation, couples in soulmate relationships will mess with your head a lot. You see these couples working together, helping each other, and you think you can help your divine masculine in the same way or that you need a soulmate instead because it looks easier.

One day, in a healthy union, you will be able to share some of that, but in separation, it is you and you alone. The strong connection between you will drive both of you to heal just as it did with me and as you saw in Neil's story.

Another thing to remember about a divine masculine who's running is that your love is not something they feel they deserve. You've most likely seen this in yourself when you picked a partner who was not emotionally available over one who was. You weren't conscious that you were doing it until your twin showed this side of you to you. Then you saw even more of it when you started your healing work. They can't see that yet. This is why we say they are asleep. And they don't want anyone else pointing it out to them, so they learn the hard way.

There is also some trauma around a divine feminine pointing out change or spiritual awakening to a divine masculine. It didn't come from you. They have encountered controlling feminine energy and wounded feminine energy their whole lives. This could have meant past girlfriends, mom, aunt, and sometimes even a big sister. Wounded feminine energy can come across as manipulation, nagging, or not giving them any freedom to be who they want to be. This causes them to people please with these current/former parts of their lives. In essence, they become someone they are not to keep the peace. This is a coping mechanism learned from childhood and carried on the way into adulthood. Your normal reaction when they begin to get quiet or run is to text them several long paragraphs explaining why they need to love you, or you work diligently to ensure they see your side of things. Instead of seeing you care, they only feel a trauma of the wounded feminine control they experienced before and come to resent you.

The universe not only wants them to wake up to this, but at the same time, you were joining with the wounded feminine energy just by chasing alone. You've seen enough people say, 'I don't chase, I attract.' That needs to be your mantra while you heal these wounds around why you think you need to work so hard for love. Do NOT feel shame around this ever. This is a common problem that keeps divine feminines stuck. Just because you had a parent you had to labor away to get any sort of love from, which got planted in your subconscious, does not mean that it needs to remain a pattern. You don't need to make it easy for your divine masculine. It is literally in their biological makeup to protect you and make you feel safe. Programming of shit THEY learned growing up is the only thing keeping them stuck, and the ego reinforces it behind the scenes.

In one of my EMDR sessions, I got an absolute gold nugget of wisdom. You do not need to take on other people's stuff. When you are still carrying childhood trauma with you and repeating patterns that don't serve you, you automatically put yourself at the bottom of the situation and other people before yourself. Another person's problem is not yours.

Let's just recap some things about the Divine Masculine:

- You cannot wake them up; the universe only does this
- There are lessons & experiences they must go through before stepping into divine union
- You can't put a timeframe on this
- During separation, take time to learn compassion & unconditional love for them
- Contacting them will only delay the process
- Contacting them means you are still in your unhealthy masculine form of chasing
- Give them space to step into their divine masculine so they can feel what that means to them rather than feeling they were manipulated into it by someone else
- They will approach you when they are ready
- When they contact you, take things slow, step back and observe whether they have awakened

- Even though your divine masculine is your soul, you must separate yourself from their issues and allow them to own them

- They are convinced that their karmic vices, be it addictions, work, another romantic interest, or family, is the experience they currently want to be in. They are only fighting themselves by pushing you away and going towards these other things. You have to set them free to see for themselves that these other options are mistakes

- Trade control for faith – that's the only way you win

- Never try to make assumptions about what you think the divine masculine is doing or what they are feeling. Odds are, you are wrong. You can only trust what you are channeling from your/their spirit team.

CHAPTER ELEVEN

UNION WITH YOUR COUNTERPART

Think of harmonious union as a delay, not denial. It will come at the right time in the right way. Everything is a risk between twin flames...the DF risks waiting for him, and the DM risks being vulnerable enough to return to something he is unsure of.

I know it might be tempting to skip all the other chapters and come straight to this one, but let me say this: If you didn't or don't read all the chapters before this, this chapter won't matter—end of story. Having a future with your counterpart depends only on you at this point. Somatic healing work, inner child work, being comfortable with being alone, setting boundaries and sitting with them, healing codependency, yet practicing vulnerability and mastering the divine masculine and feminine energies are all necessary pieces. Without working on all of these, you will fail reunion, and the runner will run again. It can be difficult in the beginning to find the desire to work on all this, but I guarantee that your future self is counting on you and believes in you—the same with your spirit team. Just have patience with yourself. So, what if you are in separation for a few years? It may sound devastating now, but you will find that the devastating part seems to disappear after going through the steps and the experiences. This is because you healed the parts inside you that made you feel like you couldn't live without your twin. You are free now, and when your twin comes back, it is because they wanted to, not because you asked. It's only natural for them to choose, with their free will to want to contact you and then be in union with you. You both have to be free in order to come together. That is the yin and the yang playing together. It is the masculine and feminine fully balanced. The runner and the chaser are no longer seen.

When you come into a 3D harmonious union, this stuff will not exist anymore. You aren't going to trigger each other every day. Make sure you have read chapter 3 on why separation is a blessing, not a punishment. You must do these things for yourself before even being able to consider union. Until you live for yourself and yourself only for a little while, until you go through the ego transformations, you won't feel it, you won't KNOW it.

Some twinflame coaches say to hold back your energy; love, sexual and otherwise, from your twinflame, while in separation. This is still a form of manipulation. If you are still holding something back in 3D in order to get something from them, you haven't healed that part of you, and you are still not practicing unconditional love. But balance requires boundaries as well. If you don't want to participate with their energy invitation that day, you need to say no. If you want to receive that love that day, you say yes. But never under any circumstance are you saying yes or no to get something in return. This is all practice.

If you know what a relationship should look like, you can start practicing that today. You need to search deep in your heart chakra for this (not through matrix-defined love). Communicate with your counterpart by talking to them when you are alone. Pretend this is the real thing. Their higher self is waiting for you to pass the tests. They are so proud when you step into this place of real love.

When you meditate, start introducing some heart chakra meditations. Invite your counterpart's higher self to sit with you through this meditation. You should begin to feel part of this and go through the higher self to your counterpart in the 3D. I'm not saying they would be able to acknowledge this, but they will feel it. It will be small, but every bit matters. If you are provided love from them during these meditations, practice how you receive it. We as divine feminines have usually had trouble receiving love, whether due to our lack of trust or maybe because no one ever showed it to us before. The masculine's role is to give you love. You've wanted them to do this for a long time, right? Exactly. You need to be ready to open like a flower and let it in. You don't need to worry about returning it at this moment. Just receive. This is one of the hardest things to do, and it will require patience and practice.

Be vulnerable with your counterpart in these experiments. If you have intimate time while thinking of them, can you tell them what you would want them to do? Even in non-intimate times, can you reveal parts of yourself you never have before? Can you tell them things you've never shared with anyone? Everything you do with your counterpart should be done in the heart and never in the ego. This is why the twinflame journey is so freaking hard. It is asking you to go somewhere you're just not used to. Your higher self will not let you down. The matrix is what let you down. Your higher self has a direct line to the universe, and they've got you. You're protected here, even through the pain.

If you can't trust your counterpart now, will you be able to trust them when they return? Are you going to be so confident in yourself that you don't need to check their phone? Are you going to let them own whatever shit they still haven't resolved within?

Are you going to be ready to communicate in a divine feminine way? Look back at chapter 1, where I talk about a true divine feminine. Do you embody these things? If you are still jealous, too emotional, codependent, or expecting love the way the matrix taught you, you are not ready. You will step through these things repeatedly until your full divine feminine awakens. The universe will test you over and over again like you are a Navy Seal.

This is not the minor leagues. This is why they say this journey is not for the weak. People will say twinflames aren't real, or your counterpart will never change. They've been placed as a test. You see many feminines out there calling themselves divine feminines and then saying angry things about their counterparts and that they are going to find a soulmate. We all go through that phase; I'm not going to lie. It might be part of your story, but this chapter is about telling you these things upfront so that when you see that happening with someone else, you can catch yourself. You can stop getting drawn into that. You can stop delaying these things. It's a game, remember. You have to start seeing these things as part of the video game trying to stop you from getting to the next level.

There are things you can practice every day in anticipation of union. If you are used to doing the following, you won't have to try and fail at union. You'll already have it down, and it will come naturally.

- Every time your ego presents itself

about why your counterpart isn't contacting you or how long separation is taking, work hard to move into the heart.

• Whenever you start feeling like a victim of separation, reframe it and remember how positive separation can be. You have a chance to find yourself and live life to the fullest while others in your life are just working and sleeping their lives away.

• If anything about your twin triggers you in separation, take the opportunity to find the source of trauma around this and heal it. Is it an abandonment wound? A neglect wound? A betrayal wound? Identify it, process it, and allow it to pass through you. Each of these released will pay you back with less triggering in the future.

If you made it to this chapter in the book, you want to level up. You want to master this. You want to see your counterpart again and see who this new person will be. Like where was the person they were? Gone. Know why? The person you were is gone. Your counterpart is on this mission with you. Same soul, same mission, same soul contract, same agreement, signed as one.

The separation test between twinflames is the most intriguing and captivating of all. Because your twin is you, you love them so much. More than anyone you've ever known. You are tied to them in your heart, mind, body, and soul. The only difference between them and you is simply body/mind. And the universe is STILL asking you to choose yourself. Twinflames that are not in union, completely healed or not, always feel a calling to their twin. It comes from the heart and never dies. So, there isn't one of us that doesn't understand how you feel. We have learned that there is no easy way with the Twinflame Journey. We don't expect short separations, and we don't expect our twin to just walk back into our lives and make everything better. We've simply accepted that another person cannot fulfill us the way we can ourselves. You just begin to live that knowing and accepting every day, and it becomes a part of your life. It's nothing more than a balance — when to give to yourself and when to give to another. The giving to another aspect is much less than you think. And love is about letting the other person be free even if that means they never return.

To get an idea of what your relationship should be like in union, here are the divine feminine and masculine explained further.

In a relationship, masculine energy is expressed healthily by:

- Looking after the feminine, protecting her
- Showing unconditional love and respect for the feminine
- Supporting the feminine, even providing financially when needed
- Bringing resources and emotional security into the relationship
- In the early stages of the relationship, the masculine side is the one that does most of the courtship. This would include after separation
- Offering secure and stable attachment
- Leading the relationship with gentleness, allowing the feminine to make the decisions they wish to make
- Showing determination, logical thinking, and quick problem-solving skills

In contrast, the feminine energy is best expressed in a relationship by adopting the following behaviors:

o Allowing the masculine to provide for you and to offer you any support they wish to offer, without feeling guilty for it or becoming too entitled

o Showing him compassion and deep empathy when he makes mistakes

o Forgiving the mistakes with grace and ease

o Understanding your partner's emotional states and needs

o Using your creativity to improve the relationship

o Being responsible for good, clear communication

o Acting from the heart, healthily expressing your emotions, and encourage your partner to do the same

○

<u>AFTERWORD</u>

Thank you for taking the time to explore through this book the next step of your growth process. I invite you to interact further with me on TikTok or YouTube.

Always remember how important you are as a lightworker. Every ounce of love cancels out an ounce of hate.

I wish you nothing but love and success along your journey. I know this is a tough one, but it is equally as rewarding.

Love,
Alyssa

Made in United States
North Haven, CT
31 May 2023

37180880R00136